Exploring the Heart of Funeral Service

Navigating Successful
Funeral Communications
&
The Principles of
Funeral Service Counseling

BY
TODD W. VAN BECK

DEDICATION

This book is dedicated to my wife and companion Georgia. For many years now she has tolerated my infirmities while I have rejoiced in her graces.

TVB

CONTENTS

Part I - 17 Landmark Traits in Navigating Funeral Service Communication

Page 3 – Experiential Expertise
Page 5 – Trust
Page 7 – The Vital and Active Role of the Funeral Professional
Page 10 – Respect
Page 14 – Understanding
Page 18 – Balance
Page 27 – Humility
Page 30 – Exploration
Page 35 – Encouragement
Page 37 – Avoidable Problems
Page 40 – Time
Page 44 – Silence
Page 48 – Personal Examples Can Hinder
Page 50 – Common Sense
Page 53 – Authority
Page 56 – Forms
Page 59 – Endings
Page 61 – Navigation Questions That Funeral Professionals Ask

Part II - The Principles of Funeral Service Counseling

Page 70 - The Foundation of Funeral Counseling
Page 84 - The Wisdom and Logic of Funeral Counseling
Page 94 - Objectives in Funeral Counseling
Page 98 - The Challenges of Funeral Counseling
Page 103 - Unique Situations in Funeral Counseling
Page 109 - The Distinctive Traits of Funeral Service Counseling

INTRODUCTION

Funeral Service counseling is difficult. This fact needs to be understood at the beginning of this book. All human interactions have an element of risk, but in funeral service counseling this risk requires constant diligence and sensitivity on the part of funeral service professionals.

A career in funeral service is unique. Funeral professionals are asked to confront, on a day by day basis, some of the most distasteful and horrific occurrences that happen in communities, and they are expected to confront these very challenging situations with consistent caring, compassion, and concern. This is not an easy career.

Funeral service is even more challenging career to excel at, and yet most funeral professionals do excel in navigating and traversing the murky waters of grief and crisis communication.

Most funeral professions excel in the art form of human caring, human compassion, and human concern. A career in funeral service is so unique that many people find it unbelievable that another person would choose such a life path – but choose it thousands of us have indeed done.

A career in funeral service, and the concept of a ministry on demand are synonyms. What this means is that funeral professionals show up when called, there is no hesitation, and funeral professionals are where the action of a death crisis is unfolding. This is a ministry on demand; people in crisis demand attention.

Funeral professionals have two major responsibilities: caretaking of the dead, and caregiving to the living. Few occupations carry such serious duties and responsibilities.

This is a book is about exploring the heart of this profession. Funeral service is first and foremost a matter of the heart.

This work is organized into two sections. The first section is Navigating Successful Funeral Communications, where we will explore seventeen Landmark character traits of what I call the Great American Funeral Director. The second section is called the Principles of Funeral Service Counseling, where we will further explore the heart of this great profession.

This is a book written by a funeral professional for other funeral professionals. In reading this material it is my sincere hope that the reader will gain additional sensitivities and insights into the heart of a wonderful profession.

Let us begin.

PART 1

17 Landmark Traits in Navigating Funeral Service Communications

1. EXPERIENTIAL EXPERTISE

I have often thought, and I have often said, that most funeral professionals deserve a PhD in experiential expertise. In other words, their life knowledge really goes way beyond the standard academic degree. There is nothing comparable in the world to the experiences of the average funeral director across the globe.

Platitude or not, I believe there is deep substance in the idea that the more we quest to know about ourselves, the better we can understand, evaluate, and control our behavior - and the better we can understand and appreciate the behaviors of others. **_This is what experiential expertise is all about._** This type of deep knowledge takes time, a ton of time to bear fruit.

Such an attitude will definitely help the bereaved client family to trust us. They will know who we are, for we the funeral professionals have accepted who we are, and shall feel no need to hide behind a mask, to be a phony, or to be an arrogant snob. Most veteran funeral professionals have learned extremely well it is very important in the funeral interview to not be preoccupied with ourselves, but concentrate wholeheartedly on the client family. This skill does take time; the more you do it the better you get – or that is the idea anyway.

We can be free to listen, to attempt to understand just as much as possible, and to be genuinely interested because nothing in us gets in the way of what comes from our task - which is to build a trusting and respectful relationship with the client family that lasts. It is in the exclusive arena of human communication that truly experiential expertise blossoms.

CASE STUDY: *Years ago, I worked with a young person who had just graduated from mortuary college, and was serving their internship at the funeral home I managed in Iowa. She interviewed very well and made a great first impression, but after one month most everyone who worked in the mortuary realized that she was not devoted to funeral service. She was devoted to the drama in her "soap opera" lifestyle. Her normal day would revolve around play by play reports of her latest argument with her latest suitors, and if in the middle of her theatrics she needed to go on a death call, she actually gave every indication that she was being "put out" by having to respond to the death of a human being - one of the glaring missions of the funeral home. Her addiction to her own life dramas was so self-consuming that she even began sharing (more like boring) her theatrical life issues with people who came off the street to innocently attend a visitation or service.*

To be sure she was young, terribly young, and to be sure we had conversation after conversation about her improving, but in the end her soap opera life prevailed and she found employment in another funeral home – a place in her own words "that understood and appreciated her". The saddest part of it all here was that the potential of developing solid experiential expertise simply froze, it stopped, and it was paralyzed. Have you ever encountered any such type in our profession as this young lady?

Looking back, weighing this situation against the substance that experiential expertise in funeral service requires, I have concluded that this young lady was not derailed by her personal crises' but that she was derailed because she missed one essential ingredient concerning being a funeral professional with experiential expertise substance. **This one essential ingredient is: a genuine love of funeral service.** A genuine love of our great and beloved profession is one of the foundational bedrocks in the quest to explore the substance and meaning of the funeral expertise. Without genuine love of funeral service anyone's efforts will always be less than they could have been. When this happens it is a pity for everybody involved.

Because of the immense power that a genuine love of funeral service ***possesses*** in purity of purpose, the authentic funeral professional developing experiential expertise sees as its very antithesis, as it stellar opposite, the concept of funeral professionals possessing an out of control ego, - or like this young lady being so caught up in her own agenda that she in the end had nothing to offer others. True she was licensed, true she passed the National Board, true she passed her state law exam, but that was it. She was stuck!

Hence, the overall professional results are often that the selfish funeral professional (now there is an oxymoron – a selfish funeral director) actually ends up helping to enhance the insecure funeral professionals ego by generating a salve or a tonic for their own dysfunctional life instead of actually helping the client family make once in a lifetime decisions. ***This is*** where all this PhD in experiential expertise comes from in the first place.

This approach in pursuing the quest of the substance of the funeral expertise holds that, at its core, it is the basic human concept of selfless humble service to others. Without this, the funeral profession loses its pure, unadulterated sacredness. Without this genuine love of funeral service, the funeral experience, and the interview conference descends into an experience which might be analogous to having an appointment with H&R Block, or your insurance representative.

Trusting our own ideas and feelings constitutes another important quality of funeral expertise. To me, this type of trusting in no way entails us telling the client family what to do. Most veteran funeral professionals would not do that even should it be asked of us. Instead, this type of rare expertise centers around the funeral professional's openness, ability, and knowledge of presenting **options, alternatives, and suggestions.**

It will be valuable for us to remember that the very definition of a suggestion is when we are told about an idea that we had never thought about before. One of the new responsibilities of the contemporary funeral professional is to take on the role of the suggestion maker. People who genuinely love something or somebody usually have a myriad of suggestions on how things can be done better, more safely, more creatively, and more lovingly. Most parents understand this approach to "suggestion making" very well indeed! If you love something your experiences, your developed expertise naturally then follows the course of offering thoughts, counsel, advice, - this is an essential in funeral professional expertise.

The result of suggestion making is that because most funeral professionals possess utterly priceless experiential expertise, which cannot possibly be found anywhere else, we (you and I) have a very important and valuable story to tell, and we ought to be able to make one suggestion after another, simply based on that we have the experience, we have that priceless form of knowledge that comes from being in the trenches, being on the front lines confronting death on a hour by hour basis – this is indeed honorable experiential expertise. We need to tell our client families what we know, we always need to tell our story, we need to not be timid or shy in telling our story, and our story in and of itself, will aid us in the admirable task of moving far beyond being stuck in traditional role of the old-fashioned order taking method of making arrangements.

2. TRUST

The funeral experience can easily be viewed as being sacred, and because it possesses sacred overtones the quality and character of the funeral professional becomes of profound importance. Because of this unique situation, a pressing question is what do we bring with us as funeral professionals, inside of us, about us that may help, hinder or not affect the bereaved client one way or another? This is indeed a tough question to tackle.

The funeral professional ought to bring to the funeral interview and funeral experience just as much of our own selves as we possibly can, stopping, of course, at the point at which this may hamper the bereaved client family or deny them the help they need.

Feeling within ourselves that we genuinely wish to help a bereaved person as much as possible and that there is nothing at the moment more important to us – this I believe is priceless substance for all funeral professionals to embrace. This ability to feel within ourselves is a critical asset for every funeral interviewer to possess, particularly in such complicated social times when people's abilities and skills to connect with each other are eroded by cynicisms, mechanic communications, and suspicions of others which seem to increase with each second that ticks away. As the great thinker Alvin Toffler once said, "As technological skills go up, people skills go down." Interesting thought, is it not?

What we are exploring here is what could easily be called high substantive funeral service ideals. Most of us (myself included), simply cannot realize immediately upon reflection what this encompasses, but this natural reaction is really never a good reason not to set ourselves on the quest to try-- to try to delve into what makes a great funeral director versus what makes the run of the mill director.

When the client family perceives that we are doing our level best (this is the invisible and silent key), it will be meaningful to them and prove very helpful. They will probably take away from the funeral interview and experience, if nothing more concrete, the authentic feeling that we as funeral professionals may be trusted as a people and the conviction that we as funeral professionals respect them as a person(s).

Trust in the funeral professional by the client family, and the conviction that the funeral professional respects them, is of the greatest importance. Without *this*, to be sure, the standard old style "funeral arrangement" procedure will probably get finished, but other than this, in these terribly complicated times, little that is really positive or of a lasting impression will be accomplished.

Our saying the mere words, "I can be trusted" or "I fully respect you" will certainly not help if the bereaved client does not sense this to be true. I think it is the establishing of trust and respect that is most often referred to by those who teach and write in the field of personal relations when they speak of "contact," "good rapport" "good relationship" and "connecting". Trust and its critical importance in this connecting process, requires that we work relentlessly after getting it and keeping it.

The real good news is that funeral professionals have ample statistical information to back up the long known fact that funeral people do connect most often in a trusting and respecting manner. For years, the Gallup Poll has asked the American public to rank the top ten most ethical and honest professionals in their community and funeral directors have always been included in the Top 10 list. Not bad at all, but interestingly I have found that the audience who is most skeptical about this statistic are funeral professionals themselves!

The experience of trust has a powerful and ever present intangible aspect to it, which is determined most by the simple old-fashioned human interest you and I take in what the client family is saying and by the understanding we show of them about their feelings and attitudes.

We communicate this, or the lack thereof, constantly, by diverse and frequently subtle nonverbal cues that the client family may be more aware of than we ourselves are. Of course, our facial expressions reveal a great deal – this is nothing new. Our bodily gestures contribute to the picture – supporting, denying, confirming, rejecting, or confusing. The tone of our voice is heard by the client family, and they decide whether it matches our words or whether they are a mask that the tone of our voice exposes, whispering, "Sham, phony, or beware!" For better or for worse, we are definitely exposed to the client family, nearly everything we do or leave undone is noted and weighed.

And so we come back to ourselves. What of ourselves do we bring to the funeral interview and experience? Oddly, we are the only known in the entire funeral equation. We cannot do anything about our bereaved client families – they are what they are. However, we can always do something about ourselves. We can always be aware and sensitive to continually improving, by expanding our creative horizons, but also by being a lifelong student of our beloved profession; digesting and embracing absolutely everything and anything that has something to do with funeral service.

Here then are some common sense suggestions and guidelines, if you will, which will help the funeral director in establishing trust and respect in our sacred arrangement conferences and elsewhere.

- Communicate. Never cross-examine.
- Maintain genuinely friendly and interested attitudes. This takes work.
- Abstain from revealing your own attitude.
- Keep your personal problems out of the funeral interview
- Avoid a patronizing or scientifically detached attitude.
- Avoid gossiping or revealing confidences.
- Avoid getting rushed or giving the impression that you are pressed for time.
- Attend exclusively to the client by blocking out all outside interferences.
- Be alert to detect the feelings which the client is expressing and feeling.

This list is not a complete list, but as with all life skill improvements it is a beginning. Look at this list, explore this list, memorize the list, and see if your connection with bereaved families in the areas of trust and respect does not enter a deeper substantive level. It is worth the time and effort.

3. THE VITAL AND ACTIVE ROLE OF THE FUNERAL PROFESSIONAL

In bygone days in our profession there was a method of "arranging" a funeral which was called "the indirect method" of counseling. At the core of this funeral arranging approach the funeral director played an entirely passive role in the decision making processes that the "family" was engaged in. The result of this approach to the funeral interview was that it did not work very well. One funeral director who was a disciple of this approach once told me, "When I make arrangements, I don't even want the family to notice that I am in the room." I cannot disagree more with this type of funeral interview approach for this is another example of black and white rule making, in which the funeral professional is making all the rules. Doesn't the families' feelings and wishes need to be taken into account, need to be respected? I believe they do.

Just imagine this scenario. The bereaved family has seen one or two caskets in their entire lives. Now, today the door is opened and they are looking at twenty-one caskets, 40 urns, 20 keepsakes and they are in the room alone – absolutely alone and on their own. Do you think this type of situation creates a vulnerable and possibly high risk client situation?

Analogous to this, for a naive fellow like me, would be my wanting to buy an airplane. The airplane company representative opens up a door to the airplane hangar that has twenty one new airplanes for sale and then turns heel and leaves. For a limited guy like me, well I don't have a chance!

The reason the indirect approach flopped so many years ago is that while some funeral professionals were attracted to it, our valued client families did not like it. The indirect approach to helping I believe was created because of our professions long standing phobia concerning any type of criticism whatsoever, and our particularly high alert sensitivity about being criticized as a "high pressured sales person" or worst or all, "taking advantage of the bereaved." I understand our professions sensitivity to this, and Jessica Mitford made hay in the sunshine using and abusing this theme. However, her book was published years ago and still our addiction to wanting to please absolutely everyone, in everything, all the time, which is utterly impossible for any human being to accomplish, still haunts our great profession.

I personally would like to suggest that the reason the indirect approach to helping a family didn't work is that it relegated the funeral professional to an exaggerated passive role, and I have concluded that bereaved clients are not attracted to passive funeral directing.

I do not see the funeral professional - as the interviewer or as a presence in the funeral experience - playing a passive role, in the least. On the contrary, I perceive the funeral professional as staying active at all times. I am not implying that he/she should talk a great deal, but I am saying that he/she should make their presence and interest continuously felt – throughout the entire funeral home experience, not just the arrangement interview. The funeral interviewer is ideally active in revealing to the client family that they are indeed an interested person in the welfare of the client family. Being too passive does not have enough energy about it to convey this important communication. In fact, being passive, in reality, is as dry as a piece of unbuttered toast.

The question then is not whether the funeral professional will be of assistance, help or counsel. **In all sincerity of purpose, is the larger question this: Will my assistance, help and counsel be based on active wisdom and care, on active insight and compassion, and on active trust and respect? The operative word here is *active*.**

Primary to this vital role is that the funeral interviewer is and acts as a genuine person. As funeral interviewers we contribute of ourselves and our professional knowledge to help the client family, and to not simply display our *intellect* or our splendid personal qualities. The funeral interviewer reveals what they themselves see and understands, what they think the client family is thinking and feeling, in order to help him/her look deeper and try harder to reach his/her inner self to make once in a lifetime decisions that offer two priceless gifts in taking the journey through the valley of the shadow of death: **Peace of mind and the feeling that one has done the right thing.** The combined psychological health of these two feelings is absolutely priceless; no dollar sign can ever be attached to this – never!

Coming right down to it in our ongoing quest for substance and meaning, what do funeral professionals actually bring to the helping interview? Essentially, we bring our knowledge, experience, professional skills, the information we possess, and the resources at our command, and above all else, a genuine committed love of the profession in which we serve. It follows then that the continuous funeral student (going considerably beyond Mortuary College and the National Board) actively continually *learns* about every single aspect of the funeral service profession. This type of quality learning will result in creating the most effective professional who, by the results of their dedication to lifelong learning, will possess the most knowledge. This professional funeral person will then be able to assist family clients by offering and suggesting creative ceremonial experiences, creative help and counsel resulting in a tangible enhancement of our bereaved clients' ability to arrive at wise, valid, and satisfactory decisions.

Here are some suggestions to help us stay active in the experience of the funeral interview and funeral service in general. Ponder these, and add to them. Your time spent thinking about these four points will prove helpful in the long term.

First: Funeral professionals use themselves first and foremost. If the funeral professional is calm, understanding and clearly concerned as well as obviously wanting to be helpful, they set the stage for the response of those being served.

Second: Funeral professionals are usually and fortunately where the action is. Doing something constructive is an important way of moving people through a crisis. **Inner balance can be sustained by outer action.** Having people do things will help to confirm reality, express feelings, and gain group support;

it is never a passive experience, these important funeral standards are always in the active tense.

Third: Funeral professionals help the expression of feelings in the helping interview. The funeral professional is usually present when feelings are intense. The funeral professional within the save harbor of the funeral interview and overall funeral experience can provide the personal attitude and social atmosphere within which the appropriate deep grief feelings can be expressed and most importantly, accepted and understood.

Fourth: **The funeral professional also has quick access to items to memorialize creativity which can help the mourner's experience deeper expression and find deeper significance in the selected services and goods which are decided upon and invested in.**

The funeral professional/interviewer/arranger (last week I learned a new professional designation "Remembrance Counselor") who is keenly aware of these four simple points and who uses them in an active, not passive way will find additional foundations of worth in their communication with the client families. Bringing yourself, ***BEING IN THE THICK OF THE ACTION***, allowing for the expression of feelings, and having at your immediate access valuable remembrance and memorial items is a wonderful way to further assist our families we are privileged to service, and that is the goal, is it not – to work to further assist our client families to the best of our abilities.

4. RESPECT

Has anyone noticed that it seems that culturally the notion of respect for other human beings has changed? And not in a good way?

Not to sound negative, but it seems evident that, culturally anyway, our ability to be respectful to others is changing and has changed – and just possibly not for the good. Have you ever seen an elderly person who just can't seem to find anyone to hold a door open for them? Have you ever tried to make a lane change on the interstate and experienced numerous unmistakable non-verbal signals from other people using their finger digits? I suspect every reader knows precisely what is being addressed in this writing. I would like to suggest that one essential – there are hundreds of essentials in the funeral interview and funeral experience – but a major one, a vital one – is basic human respect.

Interestingly, I have concluded that having basic human respect is not a character trait that you can just magically develop by reading a book, or listening to a motivational tape, or even reading this book. Respect is a core character trait, and some people will never develop it and in these cynical times, some people seem to have as a source of pride that they don't respect anyone. You know, the "take no prisoner's attitude." I would humbly like to suggest that having no respect for our bereaved client families is not just dangerous, in a caring profession like funeral service, it is cruel, thoughtless and ridiculous!

Respect for the client family and their world involves a sincere interest both in them and in their world. We show this interest by the manner in which we attend to them, you know, "fuss" over them. We show respect by carefully excluding outside interference as much as possible while we are there with them and exclusively for them, and by demonstrating that what is important to them is important to us. This last sentence sounds good, in fact it sounds terribly attractive. However, concerning respect there is a glaring truth - **showing respect to the human race is not easy at times; many times it is simply near impossible.**

The insight concerning mutual respect is that we don't have to like all our client families – but we are expected to respect them, and that is most times the most difficult helping task of all, for respect means unconditional forgiving, unconditional patience, unconditional kindness, unconditional understanding and unconditional support – or at the very least, the magnanimous attempt at giving this task our best possible effort at being "unconditional". This approach to respect is the diametrical opposite of judging a client family as being "weird", a "kook", "impossible" or "high maintenance." We don't have to like them, we have to respect them.

Some thoughtful steps in respect:

1. **Accepting the Client Family**

All of us in this honored and beloved profession have thought about the important concept of **acceptance** and the role it plays in the funeral interview and funeral experience. As helping people funeral professionals cannot NOT think about acceptance. It is one of the core values that is inherent in our profession and has been a hallmark of our great profession for hundreds of years. Most funeral professionals are accepting people, but not all.

Basically, to me, acceptance of others means treating the client family as an equal and regarding their thoughts and feelings with sincere respect, equal with my own thoughts and feelings. BUT . . . **it does not mean agreeing with them; it does not mean thinking or feeling the way they do; it does not mean valuing what they value. It is, rather, the attitude that the client family has as much right to their ideas, feelings, and values as I have to mine, and that as a funeral professional, I want to do my utmost to understand their life in terms of their ideas, feelings, and values rather than in terms of my own.** In reality, this is not in the least a simple and task assignment, but it is an extremely valuable attitude to strive for.

As mentioned, such an attitude is often difficult to maintain and even more difficult to communicate when confronted with the "difficult/dysfunctional" client family, which seems to be growing in numbers year by year. The naïve concept that all bereaved client families are like the "Walton's" on television is simply a myth. The "Walton's" was a television program, complete with make-up, costumes, memorized lines, props, and predetermined life situations. The "Walton's" have ended up on celluloid which can be repeated time after time, year after year. There was nothing real about that program in the least. It is the rare American family that would mirror the ideal of the "Walton's" – they are out there, many of us wish for this type of life, but it and they are rare.

I have encountered many different family situations over the years. Some have inspired me as to the limitless possibilities of the human spirit to prevail against the greatest of odds and obstacles, and some have been so complicated, so dramatic, so dysfunctional, that I would just leave the funeral home shaking my head, and hoping that I was good enough to "get through this."

Client families may be highly emotional or highly intellectual, or the stellar opposite; they may be crystal clear to me or not; they may seem "good" to me or "bad" – or even ridiculous and incomprehensible. However, as a professional I try (and fail many times) to report to myself what I have received from the client family, and no matter what, I attempt to treat whatever they say with respect and the client family as of equal worth with myself. I don't always succeed, but I make the attempt and many times the attempt is exhausting and just flops.

Another very important aspect of acceptance is the ability to treat as a respected equal someone of another culture, race, color, or faith. This funeral professional attribute and attitude of our hearts is all the more important and magnified as we watch the globe literally shrink before our own eyes. **Acceptance does not require strong liking, but acceptance is undoubtedly impossible when strong dislike is present.** We cannot truly help a person we cannot accept and/or strongly dislike, in my opinion, and there appears little of anything anyone can do to change the perverted world view of a bigot.

The inability to accept someone may occur even when cultural differences are absent. An honest, authentic, true incompatibility of personalities may exist – I know this has happened to me, and it still happens to me. In short, in the funeral experience we should strive to be able to first and foremost accept ourselves – our ideas and feelings as well – and to act accordingly. If we accept ourselves usually accepting others becomes much easier. Our range of acceptance may or may not broaden with time and maturity, we might well be stuck, but **in the end the truth is we can help only when we can accept** – there is no way around or a detour to this helping truth in respectfully accepting another person and their feelings.

2. Genuine Liking – A Key in Creating Respectful Rapport

A genuine liking for people is a gift from heaven. We are either born with it or we are not – it is terribly difficult to fake. Those upon whom the gift was not bestowed are neither better nor worse than other people, but they do lack a trait highly valued in a helping profession such as funeral service. If our personal preferences lead us to great interest in say machines, plants, animals, abstractions, or whatever, but not to people, we should indulge and foster such preferences – but probably steer clear of funeral service. Some professions do not demand and some even exclude a genuine liking for people. However, for those of us in funeral service a genuine liking of people is essential and it is a real asset in establishing respect.

The funeral professional who genuinely likes people tends to be optimistic about humankind. They feel involved with those about them whether it is person to person or, indirectly, through service to the wider community. The genuinely liking funeral professional tends to be tolerant of people's weaknesses and foibles but are also convinced that people have it within them to act heroically and selflessly. The funeral professional who feels genuine warmth toward people likes to learn about them and their behavior, their motives and reflect upon their inner life.

The "people liking" funeral professional tends to delight in professional literature and human psychology. This type of respectful funeral professional stays clear of pettiness, gossip, and acrimony. If this funeral professionals' liking for the human race is indeed genuine, he/she usually does not have a particularly strong insecurity to be liked in return, in other words this respectful professional has learned and accepted the wisdom lesson that you cannot be all things to all people – never under any circumstances, but we can try.

CASE STUDY: *Throughout my career I have encountered some of the finest, most outstanding human beings imaginable. From this single aspect of a lifelong career I have been most blessed. One personality, one human being emerges as a true contender for the winner of Todd Van Beck's most respectful human being award, and that person was the late Mr. Ralph S. Turner. Ralph and I were good buddies and he and I spent many hours together discussing the philosophies of the world.* **Ralph Turner** *was a wonderful man and he was genuinely liked but most importantly he respected all people. Here is an example – nothing earth shattering, nothing overly dramatic, but abundantly human.*

Ralph and I were traveling together, going somewhere, and Ralph was driving. We were on a terribly busy street in Atlanta, and the traffic was horrendous. Down the street from where we were was a huge city transit bus that was trying to dodge traffic, trying to pick up passengers, trying to drop them off, and then trying in vain mostly to get back into traffic easily. The other drivers were shaking their fists at the bus driver, honking their horns, coming dangerously close to hitting the bus itself, cutting off the bus – it was just a mess, until Ralph Turner pulled up behind the bus.

Ralph flashed his headlights, and took his hand and waved the bus to pull out in front of us saying as if he was talking to the bus driver one on one "Go ahead my friend, you've had enough trouble today". I sat in the passenger's seat and was witness to a great example of simple, authentic, and free human respect take place. I looked at Ralph and said, and I quote, "Ralph, I will never be as kind and nice a person as you are." Ralph said nothing in return, and we just continued on our journey letting the bus go in front of us for the rest of our trip.

When is the last time you have had someone be that respectful to you? Here is a challenge. Go purchase small note pads, hand them out to your work associate with a small pencil, and ask the group and yourself for one week to write down every respectful gesture or action that they do with another human being. In a week have everyone read their list, and see what is the outcome? Hopefully everyone will have pages of things they did to show respect to another human being. Hopefully that is.

We live in a very cold universe at times. We live in seemingly very cynical times. We live in a world that appears to be addicted to the negative and in proclaiming the negative in every which way possible.

Basic human respect in such a complicated impersonal climate, in these particular times in history is definitely a difficult task. However, it is my firm conviction that our beloved profession has indeed encountered difficult times in our long and rich history of service to humanity, and in the end our beloved profession has always prevailed. To be sure, we have prevailed with the scars and wounds, with some warts, and blemishes, but we have prevailed.

The prevalence of our beloved profession, in the end I believe firmly, is always, and has always been attributable to the basic respectful decency of the average, typical, funeral professional who holds tight to the worthy mission of being one and at the same time the caretaker of the dead and the caregiver to the living. It is indeed an honorable calling.

5. UNDERSTANDING

Have you every poured your heart out to somebody and they did not understand you? If this has happened to you then you will understand that one of the sterling qualities in the character makeup of the helping funeral professional is to understand other people to the best of our abilities.

I am going to cover three aspects in the process of human understanding.

1. SELF UNDERSTANDING:

- <u>**The first way to start to understand other people is to understand yourself and this most times is a painful exercise in character building which usually starts with our taking a long hard look in the mirror; not an easy assignment.**</u>

The helping funeral professional ideally is a continuous student of self-improvement and reads and thinks about the human condition, about death, loss, about the values of rituals and ceremonies, about life realities and life challenges, about grief and bereavement and how their own personal life story fits into all this life-stuff. This is indeed time well spent.

Here is a very difficult question: Do you understand yourself? In fact, when I was in seminary our pastoral counseling profession Sister Elizabeth Cashman taught us that the most difficult question that any human being can ask is this: "Who am I?" Many times the answer is "I don't know."

If your answer is "I don't know" is this then a motivator to discern and introspect about your life, its meaning and your relationships with others? Does this motivate you think about how you can do better in treating others, in understanding others, and in being of service to others?

This concept is not centered exclusively around the funeral professional becoming more acquainted with their own personality per se, but it will suffice to say that of the three types of understanding we are addressing, self-understanding, self-awareness, and self-realization are the most difficult to embrace.

Personality inventories, attitude surveys, and personal assessments are on the internet in abundance and free to help jump start a beginning attempt for an individual to start answering the question "Who am I?" Another way to find out information about who you are is in simple conversations with trusted family, friends, and professional colleagues. These interactions can be an effective approach in our process of looking hard and long in the mirror. All of these avenues are readily available and for the serious life student should be taken full advantage of.

CASE STUDY: *For several years I played host to a group of nursing students who came to the funeral home I managed to take a tour. The nursing students did this twice a year. It has always fascinated me to watch people take a tour of a funeral home and the nursing students were no exception. The process is usually predictable; the group hesitantly enters the building, sometimes giggling, bumping into each other, trying to act mature, but then defy their act by laughing at inappropriate times and over inappropriate subjects.*

Then I introduce myself. Any reader who knows me knows that I am a "big boy" and have a shock of white unruly hair, and a deep bass voice; one of my speaker associates dubbed as "the voice." In other words, I am innocently intimidating – I don't mean to be, but that is the way it is, of course until people get to know my loveable personality (that is a joke folks).

The nursing students, naturally don't know or understand anything concerned with anything about our beloved profession, absolutely nothing, and even if they "think" they know something, the odds are always on the side that what they think they know is wrong. They also know absolutely nothing about me, so I know they are not looking at me as a feeling human being, but as an odd and strange fellow who is working in this odd and strange place.

So off I begin, and you know there is absolutely nothing I love to talk about more than funeral service and just how bloody great this career path truly is.

I move them across the threshold of funeral anxiety into the world of funeral interest, and once that happens watch out, because the young nursing students, as most people do, move quickly into an arena of active interest and then questions start coming fast and furious. I believe this is the premier reason why funeral home tours are so important. It is the best way to move anxious people from funeral and death anxiety to funeral and death interest. ***I firmly believe my friends that since the death rate is a perfect 100% this activity is always a good thing!***

I have also discovered on these tours that while the different groups are interested in embalming, caskets, vaults, and such memorial items, what they really are interested in are themselves, and their own personal understanding of the world of death, dying, bereavement, grief, and their personal relationship to this reality, and how it makes them feel. ***And this is always a good thing, and happens most authentically inside of any funeral home anywhere on the globe.***

The nursing professor always requires each student to write an assessment of this experience, and truth be told the nursing students' written words, after their experience of standing in the presence of death is simply astounding to read, and this happens on tour after tour after tour. Their writing reflect their new found introspection, discernment and maturity concerning the most certain event in their life after their birth – their death. The giggling has stopped and true understanding has happened. It is a marvelous thing to witness and be a part of.

2. <u>UNDERSTANDING OTHERS</u>

- The second way of understanding is to understand the other person, not through the eyes of others, but through our own eyes. Since this is the method by which we most frequently understand others, it deserves further scrutiny.

When I understand you or fail to understand you, I use the resources at my own command – no one else's: my perceptual apparatus, my thinking, my feeling, my knowledge and my skills. I understand you or do not understand you in terms of myself, my life space, my internal frame of reference. If we do not speak the same language – although we may both be speaking English – I may not understand you at all. This happens constantly and is most often the causal agent for wars between nations, relationship breakup, and interpersonal conflicts.

In brief, when I understand you or when I do not, it is in terms of my background, my experience, my imagination. Most often, I suppose, we cannot do otherwise and at best, we can only be aware that this is what we are doing. Even a sensitive awareness of what is going on is a great start in improving our ability to understand others. Let me give a short example to clarify: "I don't understand you. It's so hot in here, and yet you keep complaining that it's cold." This is simple and obvious. I cannot understand that you are cold when I am warm – this "stuff" happens constantly in human interactions.

Interestingly, for our profession grief is universal human emotion. It is true that "pain is pain and grief is grief" the world over. Hence, one binding connection that members of our great profession possess that eludes many other vocations, is that no matter what, you and I can probably understand the most difficult person by connecting with them in empathetic grief counseling, and we are very good at this.

While this deep connection is a valid and real possibility, many times some in our profession continue to tend to understand these deep emotions only in terms of themselves instead of the person expressing them. **Authentic understanding of another person takes a tremendous amount of good old fashioned work, and this is also just possibly why veteran funeral directors seem to possess magical understanding of a myriad of grief situations because they have just worked at understanding this emotion and communicated with people experiencing this painful emotion for so long.**

Understanding another person can be exhausting. For this reason lazy people usually fail at understanding others very successfully. The most un-ambitious expression which indicates a lazy person's interest in working to understand another is this phrase: "I don't care." Ever heard that one?

Such an internal attitude as "I don't care" is anathema to everything which we hold near and dear in our heart concerning our love of funeral service. Here is a haunting question: Have you ever heard anyone in funeral service say "I don't care?"

Another helpful and wise step in our understanding of others is that if we do not understand people, we may well want to find out what is causing the barrier. In some rare instances in funeral service, we may have to accept lack of communication as inevitable with the result being that the client family leaves and engages another funeral home – this happens, but fortunately it is rare.

As distasteful as the "lost call" can be, at least we can attempt to cope with what we do not understand in losing a client family and take some comfort in the fact that if the family had stayed it might well have been worse with days of repeated failings to communicate and hence, understand them time after time which results in stress and turmoil for everyone involved. In a very real sense true understanding of certain situation results in the blunt realization that this client family in truth should be using another funeral home.

The upside to awkward situation is that although the barrier (why the client family left) will not have been removed with their absence neither will it have been fortified. The situation of the lost client in most funeral careers is so distasteful and stressful that the third way of understanding deserves our utmost attention.

3. UNDERSTANDING WITH ANOTHER PERSON

- The third way to understand another person is the most meaningful but at the same time the most demanding. It is to understand *__with__* another person.

This calls for putting aside everything but our common humanness and with it alone, trying to understand with the other person how they think, feel, and see the world about them. This way of understanding means it is ALL about the other person – it is selfless, pure and simple.

This means ridding ourselves of our internal frame of reference and adopting the other person's internal frame of reference without any mental reservation or compunction.

This skill is rare indeed. Here the issue is not to disagree or agree or even like or dislike the person but to **understand what it is actually like to be that other person.** This sounds quite simple, though in reality, it is extremely difficult - if not impossible - to achieve in life, with years of practice and discernment, let alone have it present within the boundaries and limits of the funeral conference.

Feeling what it is actually like to be another person requires training and extended education in the skills and procedures of the empathetic relationship. Customarily this skill is relegated to licensed therapists who form and maintain longtime working relationships with their clients.

6. BALANCE

We don't think about this much but in a real sense the funeral experience, the funeral interview is full of phases, divisions and stages. This is very important for without phases, divisions and stages the funeral experience, and the funeral interview gets stuck.

If forward movement in the overall funeral experience is absent, this usually indicates that we are stuck and when a funeral director gets stuck, this most often results in there being painfully slow movement forward; it becomes an exercise in verbosity, an exercise in exhaustion for both the funeral director and the family clients, and the worst consequence of all it ends up being an abuse of our client family's time. What we do is critically important, but for us to think that the funeral experience is the **only** thing a bereaved client has to do is an exaggeration of our importance.

A word of clarification. When I write about a funeral director getting stuck, I certainly don't mean to say that there ought to be the rush on time, not in the least. Also, I don't mean to communicate that being stuck means our doing or saying nothing. In fact, being stuck in the funeral arrangement conference/interview or in the general funeral experience is usually not because the funeral director is not talking, it is precisely the opposite; **the funeral director is wasting the family's time because he/she is talking way too much.** This case study should illustrate my point.

CASE STUDY: *Most of my readers know that I just like funeral directors. I have always liked funeral directors, and it makes no difference who they are or where they come from. I like talking with them, I like working with them, and most of all I like learning from them.*

Early in my career I was blessed by being mentored by some mighty fine funeral directors, and these great ones all had one stellar characteristic in common – they were kind hearted people. Looking back it is clear that most of these great personalities weren't great business people, they didn't know a profit and loss statement from a pipe organ, they were better than that: **they were great funeral people.**

Having a kind heart in my humble opinion is the one of the major keys of service in our great and beloved profession. I have had this philosophical opinion about the DNA of funeral service for many years. In the end, all funeral service is local, and is a matter of what is in the funeral directors heart. Nothing, absolutely nothing that promotes permanent good in our great profession happens until FIRST something good happens in a funeral directors heart.

Of course, as we will soon see, having a good heart does not equate into having inner balance.

Not too many years ago I was involved with a consulting project with a large funeral home operation. The company was very old and highly respected. The family was very proud of their heritage (the firm opened in 1888), and this particular funeral family got along, they liked each other.

On the staff of this funeral home was one particular gentlemen. The moment I was introduced to him I liked him. He had a cherub-like baby face, a great big welcoming smile, he dressed immaculately, exhibited good taste all the time, and he had brilliantly polished shoes. He had been at this funeral home for decades.

The staff uniformly liked him (now there is a miracle), he was meticulous on funerals, and he was an outstanding embalmer. He even told me that he still mathematically figured out the HCHO demand for each and every decedent he was privileged to embalm!

However, for all his outstanding characteristics this funeral professional regularly got stuck in making funeral arrangements, and as a consequence he would innocently offend many of the families he was asked to serve.

Routinely, family satisfaction surveys would arrive and this funeral director had negative comments which showed a trend in his unbalanced approach to his professional responsibilities. Here are a few of the comments that I personally read: "Great guy, but WOW can he talk!" "I was ready to shoot myself!" "I thought we would be in and out in short order, hell Dad pre-arranged everything!" "I know he was trying to help us, but please tell him to talk less and help us more by finishing instead of going on and on and on!" Here was the most brutal comment: "I was ready to blow my brains out!" Here was the most creative comment: "Listening to him talk was like attending an endless insurance seminar."

You get the idea. This gentleman, this kind-hearted man was out of balance because he was just talking too much. He didn't have a mean bone in his body, but yet his inability to guide the client's funeral experience was stymied because he just kept talking. No matter how sincere he was in his heart, the comments on the family satisfaction survey's proved beyond a shadow of a doubt that first, what he was rambling on about was overdone, and second the family clients had concluded that after a while their time was being abused.

In the end this kind hearted funeral director was just too set in his ways to change, and the owners of the funeral home were too nice to reprimand him out of respect for his good points, so in the end the funeral owners simply waited it out, tolerating the negative comments, until this really nice funeral director retired.

This is only one example of being stuck by having an unbalanced character flaw. Out of balance attitudes and activities can happen on funerals, on cremation activities, burials, receptions, any myriad of activities which go on in funeral homes. Most every activity in a funeral home, to be optimally effective, requires forward movement in both time and space.

It seems many times in the process of learning our inner balance of helping people (which is the premier mission of the funeral profession) that the pendulum swings in an exaggerated movement from way too far on this side and way too far on the other side. Much of emotional health is to be found when we discover how to live in the middle of the tensions created by the opposite in our lives.

Not to sound impossibly inconsistent, but an example of this exaggerated zig zag movement would be the opposite of the funeral director who gets stuck in talking too much, to the funeral director that makes the funeral experience so rapid and swift that it is very difficult for a client family to determine just where one phase of the overall funeral experience ends and the next one begins.

One quick conclusion that we can make right now is to say, given what I have just shared, it is clear as a bell that being an effective funeral professional is **NOT AN EASY TASK!** So what to do? I don't have the total answer, but here are some humble thoughts.

THE SYMMETRY OF BALANCE: ONE OF THE KEYS OF SERVICE TO OTHERS

Balance then is our watchword. Not too much, not too little. That my friends is a mighty difficult assignment and an almost impossible task, but we can try.

I would like to humbly suggest that in locating our illusive balance in life is more magnified right now, today, in the present, in our current funeral world, than it has ever before been in the long and impressive history of our great profession. Why? **For the simple reason that things seem everywhere seem to be so unbalanced, so unstable, so confusing when a loved one dies and when death occurs.**

I would like to make clear that I am not telling other funeral professionals how they should do things or not do things; I am not that insightful. This work is devoted to exploring the nuances, the tiny little aspects in the big picture of the overall funeral experience and the funeral interview. It is not a **"How to Guide" that you can purchase for $19.95 on Amazon or the Home Shopping Network, and if you buy two, the second one is free, and I will toss in a free lip brush and trocar tip with your order if you call in the next 10 minutes.**

Most all funeral professionals, I have concluded, are well versed in the techniques of the funeral interview and implementing and overseeing funeral rituals in their own respective communities. Clearly the public likes funeral directors. However, is it not a good idea to just once in a while, every now and then, take time to review and think about what we are doing? Anyway that seems a good idea to me. Let us proceed.

As obvious as this thought might be on the surface I would suggest that one aspect of bringing more balance in our professional work is in the important initial stage of a funeral ceremony or a funeral interview. At the beginning. I would like to suggest, that while you and I might well know why the clients are sitting there, in these turbulent days this might not always be the case. Because of this, I would suggest that to balance out the initial phase of the entire funeral experience the matter about which the funeral professional and client family are meeting should be stated. This seems so obvious, but I have discovered that some family clients are so confused, so grieved, and so distracted that they don't know precisely why they are with us, nor do they know what they want, or what to expect, or what to do, and as we will see, this confusion can only exacerbate itself because in this state of chaos many clients end up changing their minds, then changing them again – which represents no balance at all. **We are the educated professionals that need to show empathy with each bereaved client, in other words, how would we feel if we had just lost our child or spouse yesterday?** I know this sentiment has been expressed this same way a thousand times, but I believe it is a sentiment that is worth repeating, and repeating, and repeating, for one solid reason: what would the funeral service profession be without sentiment?

Because of this contemporary reality in our profession, funeral professionals don't have to talk a great deal, but they do have to listen and lead a great deal. Balance is easily composed of what I call **"Listening Leadership."** Listening and leadership go hand in hand and this is not an easy assignment.

Let us return to our talkative kind hearted funeral professional. His family surveys were needlessly negative because he was talking so much he couldn't lead. He literally ran out of time, and hence was unable to listen intently to the client's inner most wishes and directions. He flopped at offering his valued clients all the options and alternatives available because he spent an hour on vital statistics alone. Vital statistics are critically important, but are they the **CENTRAL CORE** of the funeral ceremony and interview experience?

The challenge of balancing out **Listening Leadership** in helping others is that it seems a valid observation in our complicated culture to say that many people don't like to be led and resent the notion of being led. In other words, many contemporary people are very attracted to the idea of "being the master of their own destiny", "doing my own thing", or "I don't need any advice." This contemporary attitude is a far distance to what bereaved families used to be like, when they basically followed the funeral professional's guidance and leadership with great devotion. Because of this current situation the impact and important component of listening while leading is of the utmost importance in our quest for balance in being of service to others.

My personal experiences have taught me through the school of hard knocks that while these nice people who are "independent thinkers" who resist and resent that notion of being led, are the very same people who can easily put the funeral director in a very vulnerable and awkward position. While they might resent the notion of our leading them, helping them, suggesting to them or resent the very idea of the representative imagined authority of a professional individual, just let something happen in their experience with us that because they really don't know what they are doing ends up causing them embarrassing blunders because their inability to listen to us, and we all know who these "independent thinkers" these good people who "don't want our help" or "we will take care of most of this on our own" will quickly blame. They blame us!

So, my friends in funeral service, if we (you and I) don't step up to the plate and balance this confusion out by offering gentle guidance, suggestions, and working in the service vineyard by planting a myriad of creative suggestions in their brains that they may not have ever considered before, or nurture and germinate a new funeral service idea, the consequences can well turn out unpleasant for you and I in the blink of an eye.

This then my friends is indeed a sticky wicket which confronts our profession in the 21st Century. Here then is the present day conundrum that confronts funeral professionals; bereaved clients don't want direction, but then they do want direction. Bereaved clients don't want advice, but then they do want advice. Bereaved clients don't like suggestions, but then they want suggestions. Does this situation strike any of the readers as being out of balance? We expect the bereaved family to be out of balance, but what if the funeral profession is out of balance? What will happen? Well, just possibly a negative family satisfaction survey.

In order to further analyze inner balance it might be helpful to put the overall funeral experience, both the ceremony and interview into a system of phases. It works like this:

The initial phase in the funeral interview starts immediately after the death. This phase can cover a myriad of issues but generally centers around the decisions that the client family needs to address concerning the death of another human being, the practical decisions concerning the legal disposition of a decedent, and ceremonial creativity. Likewise, in the overall, big-picture funeral ceremony the initial phase centers on where people need to be, at what time, who is doing what, how long will this last and again many other possible activities.

These two beginnings, or initial phases in both the actual funeral ceremony and funeral interview, calls out for a concentrated balance from the funeral professionals perspective in order to bring calm and trust from people who may feel they know that they know, but in reality, they don't know that they don't even know what to do. This distinct happening is seen exhibited in people who have attended scores of funerals for "other" people, and possibly attended scores of ceremonies in your location. It is now clear that in this all important initial phase of a funeral ceremony and/or a funeral interview, balance is created more by what the funeral professional does, how they led, how they listen, than what they say.

In today's current culture of fast lane living, in keeping up with the Jones', I have found to my utter fascination that the funeral interview and funeral ceremony may not even deal with the "traditional" matters of practical information taking, with the funeral professional asking primarily closed questions, and being most preoccupied with instructional procedural aspects that were given by the client family. While taking and following family instructions is still a valid and important segment of the funeral ceremony and interview, certainly it is not overstated that this "balance" in the funeral professional's interactions with the contemporary client has most definitely been tilted.

Historically, these "procedural" matters were so high on the agenda of the tasks of most funeral professionals, asking for and receiving instructions from family clients, I concluded many years ago that funeral directors were in reality more like high functioning organizational specialists instead of mere order takers – which I still believe to be valid today.

However, and this is a big however, in today's world, the modern customer seems more skeptical, more cynical, and more distrusting. Because of this, the standard historic instruction of receiving and acting upon is being replaced by a new environment which now includes- from the consumers point of reference (or the lack thereof) - a myriad of other unknown and unexpected points that can easily arise and hence, needs to be confronted by the funeral professional in both the funeral ceremony and interview.

CASE STUDY: *As many of my readers already know the first funeral home I worked at, the place which gave me my start was the Heafey & Heafey Mortuaries in Omaha, Nebraska.*

At this particular time in history Heafey & Heafey was primarily built on a clientele that was associated with the Roman Catholic Church. It is not that Heafey's didn't do Protestant funerals, it was just that we didn't do many of them.

I well remember the first funeral masses I assisted on seemed to me to be set in stone. The rituals were set, solid and secure. It seemed also that they were basically generally speaking the same in every Catholic Church in Omaha.

One of my jobs during funerals was to make sure that the three candles on each side of the casket, up by the chancel rail, six total were in place right after the casket was placed, and the bereaved family had been seated by Mr. Heafey.

I really enjoyed that responsibility, and I took that responsibility very seriously. Also I was good at it. Of course looking back it wasn't that difficult of a job to do!

I had never heard of Vatican Two. I didn't know what it was, where it was, or who was doing it, but in short order there was unbalance in my life as a funeral assistant.

*One sunny Omaha morning we pulled the procession up in front of a Catholic Church in North Omaha, everything was running smoothly, until I walked up to the front of the sanctuary and low and behold **THERE WERE NO CANDLES!***

I froze, looked at Mr. Heafey, and he gave me "the look" which always nonverbally communicated the message "you do nothing, and get out of here." I received that look from him hundreds of times.

Naturally most of the readers will immediately recognize that the changes, which certainly created a sense of being unbalanced, in working a Roman Catholic funeral had been put into place.

It is risky to fiddle with the ancient, and historic traditions of people. However, when they get fiddled with they never ever go back to where they were. Let's keep that in mind as we continue.

What happened to me on that funeral in North Omaha created a highly uncomfortable situation in the form of surprises. Then there were more surprises which created an atmosphere that simply cried out for inner balance concerning my performance on a funeral in a Catholic Church in North Omaha, and hence in my interactions with people.

This case study happened almost half a century ago, and I now can make a testimony that the surprise I encountered in North Omaha, the unbalanced tense feeling it created in me has actually never stopped happening, and from my vantage point given the complications of living life in the 21st century, I don't see the surprises in our beloved profession stopping anytime soon, and for this premier reason our serious consideration of inner balance I want to suggest is critically important!

There was a time, not long ago when the funeral interview and ceremony was set, solid and secure – both experiences seemed basically to be written in stone. However, today in this nonstop world made up of hectic times of rapid fire changes, what seemed in the past as being so central to a client family and then hence so central to us can, and routinely does diminish or vanish altogether in a New York second in importance. Only to be quickly and randomly replaced by "people" with other ideas, wishes, instructions, and creative imaginations which are today of importance to our client family and which just a years ago were not important in the least.

Exploring and identifying the inner balance of the modern funeral professional has as a great part of that task the mammoth assignment of keeping up with what is going on in funeral service, not just in the USA, but globally.

I suspect that many contemporary funeral professionals, my friends and associates, do what I do many times by walking away from a funeral ceremony or interview experience, or both just scratching our heads and silently and privately asking this haunting question "where in the world did they get that idea from?" **In other words, in these turbulent times in the funeral world, anything can happen.**

I hope that I have made my case concerning the importance of exploring inner balance.

To conclude, I would like to offer some common sense ideas concerning how to raise the bar concerning our quest for inner balance. I am not a psychologist, or a very insightful human being, but as a true lover of this great profession I hope the reader will find these thoughts helpful. I know I sound like a parrot many times but out of pure conviction is not this worthy ideal the ethical goal behind all funeral experiences and interviews – **funeral professionals following the noble goal of simply being helpful to another human being?**

Sometimes we might have made something that is in reality very simple very complex, because the high nobility of being helpful to another human being is most often just as simple as you and I just getting a box of Kleenex, sitting down and listening to a story of loss and grief.

LISTENING: IT IS HIGHLY IMPORTANT FOR INNER BALACE

Some of the readers may know that my hobby is not fishing, nor woodworking, nor sports, no none of these. My hobby is the study of the lives of the Presidents of the United States, and I must confess that I have never tired of this interest. People who know me and find out this odd and unusual hobby almost always ask "Who was your favorite President?" Well of course, I immediately name President Lincoln, but then I surprise most everyone by sharing the second favorite President on my list: Calvin Coolidge.

Calvin Coolidge was nicknamed "Silent Cal" and with good reason. He just never talked much but listened intently all the time. President Coolidge had a quote which he used frequently, which I have often thought I should have remembered many times in my life, here it is: **"You will never be asked to repeat something you haven't said."**

I have discovered, not perfectly of course, but I have seen it work; if we implement honest listening and sincere absorption of what we have heard the conclusion is almost universal that honest communications will happen, and honest communication seems to me is the key aspect of finding balance in internal conditions that follow each other in forward movement of the substance of the funeral ceremony and interview. Our core substance of inner balance is this: **Being honest with ourselves so that we may be honest with our clients.**

I well remember when I started doing my own funeral interviewers and funeral ceremonies I was, most often, out of inexperience and immaturity, so concerned with just getting the basic required essential details correct, trying to simply understand all that was going on, trying to just get through the funeral interview - and then on top of all that get through the funeral ceremony - that I really did miss the fact that I had not connected with the client family.

In fact today, 40 plus years later, I look back with true pity for the first 200 or so client families I "helped" for I am now predicting that at least 50% of them are still seeking some type of psychiatric care or intervention in some manner or another at some institution or other. Others may claim perfection – not TVB!

I know this personal account that I have just shared concerning my own honest vulnerability in my own shaky confidence in making funeral arrangements and conducting funerals certainly happened to me when I started out and truth is sometimes it still does. There are no guarantees in the funeral interview process, or in the funeral ceremony experience but I do know that as time passed, and as I listened to veteran funeral directors my inner balance did indeed improve and mature – and what a blessing that was in my life.

7. HUMILITY

Being out of balance in our careers for whatever reason or cause, in our early years anyway, is most often predictable and understandable to all in our profession. It harkens the ancient mentor apprenticeship system, which is still alive and well in many states as part of the final training of up and coming funeral directors and embalmers. If the truth be told, we have all been there, the feeling of being insecure, or wanting recognition, or desperately wanting to be liked and approved of.

Do you remember when things that today mean nothing to you, at one time in your life were highly significant and important? I do. I remember I desperately wanted to drive the hearse. I wanted to take the big black car down Dodge Street in Omaha and have everybody turn, stare, and look at ME! Hey! Look at ME! Today when I have to drive a hearse, and the operative word is drive, I spend the bulk of the experience trying to get the bulk of TVB in and out of the vehicle and cussing all the way, promising to go on a diet as soon as I park the blasted vehicle back in the garage. Remember those experiences?

However being stuck in immature, unbalanced, awkwardness, centering on the "I" instead of the "Thou" is in the end is not beneficial to anyone if it continues. What is called for interestingly in these instances is a good old-fashioned dose of humility. When I was driving the Heafey & Heafey funeral coach down Dodge Street I didn't have a humble cell or molecule in my body.

Humility most always redirects the focus from us to others, from the "I" to the "Thou." It almost always redirects our unbalanced notions about life and others to more mature balanced notions about life and others, and this is a priceless and tremendous asset in creating a meaningful funeral interview and a meaningful funeral ceremony.

Gentle humility, coming from a discovered deep inner conviction in our search for inner balance, and then in turn being authentically humble with others is a highly valued skill in literally every aspect of funeral service excellence.

Humility is not easy, and it takes time to develop. A good first step, a good starting point for us, in this development of inner balance leading to humility is perhaps**: to realize first and foremost, with genuine humility, what we say is generally much less important than we think it is.**

The wonderful aspect of this simple first step is that it is free. You don't have to pay a therapist to find it, you don't have to purchase a myriad of self-help books and tapes to get it, you don't have to attend one seminar after another (although great work is accomplished with all this) - all you have to do is think about the last highlighted statement and honestly conclude as to where you honestly fit?

Do we really think everything that comes out of our mouths has to rank with the content and thought of say the "Gettysburg Address" or the "I Have a Dream" speech? Of course it doesn't, that is utterly ridiculous – Abraham Lincoln's and Rev. Dr. Martin Luther King, Jr.'s are rare and special in the world. However, tell this to people with unbalanced, out of control arrogance and it probably will be difficult for them and they may well not understand this truth of this – at first anyway.

When I began my career in funeral service I, in truth, was so unsure of myself that I felt the need to prove how confident and important I was. When I started out in my career in the funeral service I was so insecure and yet so enthusiastic at the same time that my own eagerness to do everything, to be everything, to all people across the globe, or well in Omaha anyway, got in the way and I missed for way too long the asset of being humble – and got into a bunch of trouble to boot!

Prideful enthusiasm can over time, if it doesn't change, be fatal in trying to humbly help people, and once again, needlessly, the tremendous human qualities had for the benefit of being of service to others just vanishes. What a pity!

Looking back at my own beginning work in funeral service, I know I made many embarrassing and foolish mistakes, and even today I know of no easy remedy for this except inner patience and awareness of our self by constantly looking inward to locate our inner balance, then to lock onto that balance, nurture and feed that balance, and then never let go of it - which over the veil of time, will create the high watermark in how we are evaluated as to the quality of our success as a human being.

Here is some good news concerning the inner balance which humility brings. In our great profession we truly do have the brutally honest assessor, a commandant of truth, the final assessor, the judge, jury and executioner all wrapped up into one or several highly significant persons. This one person is a person who most often will, without hesitation or mental reservation, put us in our places whether it hurts our feelings, or our pride, or even whether we are genuinely listening to them or not.

Even in the most obnoxious and ridiculous example of an out of control, ego maniac funeral director who is the poster child for a total lack of humility, who is a person who is annoyingly insecure or immature cannot in the end prevail against this person(s).

Who is this person or person(s) you ask? Easy answer: it is the family client(s). And I have discovered in my own life and usually to my own deep chagrin and deep embarrassment this unblemished truth: **The client family, one way or another, will usually set us straight.**

This can sting, can hurt, can be brutal, but in the end, for the self-improvement of our great profession this resource is an absolute blessing. In fact, this is really something my "talkative", really kind funeral director simply never figured out. The truth serum (the client family) told him, and the owners of the funeral home time after time what they thought, and through just not listening, too much pride, not enough courage, well an unfortunate unbalanced situation arrived that was only corrected with this funeral directors retirement ditto exit.

Naturally most of everything I have been writing about is more a developed art and skill than it is a science or hard and fast theory and for this reason alone this "stuff of life" is difficult to teach. There is no guarantee that when you search balance that it will be successful, but not to search can be worse. So what to do? Here are some thoughts in closing.

As it is with every artist they must discover his or her own style and the tools with which he or she works best; so it is in our quest for substance and meaning of inner balance for the funeral professional and hence then of the funeral interview and the funeral ceremony.

Styles usually, and fortunately for humanity, matures with experience, discernment, and reflection. Individual styles are special things. Individual styles, I have concluded have made some of the greatest funeral professionals I have ever encountered.

Your quest is to develop your own inner balance which will change your style and most often for the better. I am not interested in you adopting my style or vice versa, but in this writing I am very much interested in stimulating you to develop and reflect upon your own style; you own inner balance; your own humility; your own maturity.

There is no magic dust or magic potion to guarantee this will ever happen, **but there is interestingly one single magic bullet to insure that at least something will happen – and that single magic bullet in our beloved profession is YOU – YOU the funeral professional.** The nobility of the funeral service profession does not revolve around the dead, it doesn't in the end even revolve around the bereaved; the nobility of our great and beloved profession revolves upon what character resides in the mind and soul of every funeral professional on the face of the earth. I believe this with every ounce of blood in my veins and air in my lungs. It is a truth!

Earl Nightingale, the popular radio commentator once gave a program called "The Strangest Secret." The programs name caught my attention. Here is what Mr. Nightingale said was the strangest secret in life: **we become what**

we think about. Sounds terribly simple doesn't it, but do not be deceived; it is not.

Here is how the strangest secret in life works: if you think long enough about being a humble person that is what you will become. If you think long enough about listening better to other people you will become a better listener. If you think long enough about being a passionate funeral professional you will become a passionate funeral professional. If you think long enough about how to help more people in your life, you will help more people in your life. Again, this sounds simple, and this is not the "think system" - this takes a ton of introspective work, but most of the greats or the greats in every line of endeavor have found this "strange secret" to be true, and embracing it makes all the difference in the world.

If you think about being a prideful, selfish person that is just what you will become, the overall idea being of course that with each thought there will be definite consequences – good and bad. This is a Newtonian law of physics, for every action there is an equal and opposite reaction.

The symmetry of inner balance, of becoming listening leaders, of possessing earned humility and the secret of just what we think about out are four powerful aspects of living and helping other through sensitive service and calls out for every person in our beloved profession to give attention, to explore, to examine and to discern.

All four characteristics are part of the overall approach which is the hallmark of quality and dedicated service to humanity, and which has been at the forefront of our professions longstanding quest for professional enhancement in being of service to others as they journey through the valley of the shadow of death.

8. **EXPLORATION**

It is fascinating to realize that in reality most experienced funeral directors use most of the psychological and counseling interviewing techniques that therapist, psychologists, pastoral counselors and clergy use every day, but just haven't given the skills a label or title The process of using exploration in the funeral interview experience is a prime example of this.

Exploring with our clients is most often the main body of the funeral interview and most of the time spent in this mutual exploring translates into a variety of important life matters, by trying to examine all aspects of the options and alternatives available and then to reach certain conclusions which are meaningful to our client families. There are some safe ways to approach the process of exploring a client family's options, suggestion, and alternatives which we will "explore" together. These approaches might not apply to every funeral professional in every circumstance, but still they are worth exploring, and they just might be valuable to you. ***Your bottom line may well depends on it.***

OUR LEARNING FROM THE PAST.

I believe that most funeral directors excel at having and using a myriad of life experiences in the funeral interview whether they are aware of this resource or not.

Intending no disparagement of any other sources (both written and spoken), I would say that you can best help yourself by using your own past funeral interviews as guideposts – thinking about them, discussing them with other funeral colleagues and supervisors, possibly even taping and listening to your own recorded interviews and those of others. In other words, systematize your life experience, and make that system part of your life-long learning.

Every funeral interview in every death situation is different (or is certainly should be), and if, as funeral interviewers, we get stuck in routine habits the consequences can be extremely distasteful to both the funeral professional, and the bereaved client family which dominos quickly into a diluted and shallow overall ceremonial and ritualistic experience – and in our profession this is **NEVER GOOD.**

I believe it is appropriate at this juncture to mention a few words about the easily untapped wisdom of the veteran funeral professional.

We live in a time that seems to worship youth, but this worshipping of the young, while trendy and attractive, has inherent risks attached and particularly when we are exploring something as important, dramatic, and sensitive as the consequences of the death of a human being, and the decisions that will be arrived at concerning what will or will not be done with that deceased human being. No Pollyanna stuff here!

In the critically important step of funeral interview exploration the veteran funeral professions have one great advantage over their youthful compatriots, and that is: the funeral road is not new to the veteran funeral professional, in fact they are still on it, and it is still taking them places. The risk of youth is they sometimes think that the funeral rules have changed, and certainly in many ways they have, but the veteran funeral director is keenly aware of the risks involved in moving too fast, too quick and in fiddling with customs, and community standards simply based in the immature notion of just changing things.

There is an old Iowa farm saying which goes this way: "Better not take the fence down before you understand why it was put up in the first place." Changing things simply for the sake of change usually translates in going from nothing to nothing.

Because of the wealth of knowledge that most veteran funeral professionals possess because they have been on the frontline for a long time, this type of wisdom needs to be shared with the youth who are entering funeral service.

CASE STUDY: *It is nice to be at a place in life where you don't have to be bashful about telling stories on yourself, and particularly stories that have a point to make about what you are writing or speaking about.*

This story is an account of one of the **many** *of bonehead mistakes that I have made in my life and career. The only comforting aspect of this story is that it happened 45 years ago, but honestly I must confess I am still making mistakes.*

I worked for a veteran funeral director who was most highly respected and beloved in our community. Looking back at his approach to our beloved profession he possessed some magnificent gifts, and one of them was he was a master at exploring with other human beings. While he never called it exploring, nonetheless he was highly skilled at asking good questions, and then being still, and let the exploring process take its course.

We were called out one beautiful summer afternoon to North Omaha on a suicide. When we arrived at the residence the Douglas County Coroner was already there, as were two police officers. Clearly the poor man had taken his own life. I hadn't been exposed to many suicides and was unnerved by what I saw and what I was asked to do – but step up to the plate I did, because I wanted to be a good funeral director.

Two nights later the poor decedent was reposing in our chapel, the casket was opened, he looked great, and the calling hours had begun.

My job was to be the attendant at the front door, which was a job I loved (back then I did anyway). I would stand there in my dark suit, trying desperately to look highly dignified, even though my chronic acne always gave me away.

The widow of the deceased was in the chapel, and she was in a very bad way. My employer had been in and out of the chapel all afternoon, and I noticed that he really didn't say much. However, the widow couldn't stop talking.

About 4:00 p.m. my employer came by and told me that he had to step out for a moment and do a personal errand. I was given strict instructions to watch my p's and q's, which was code in the funeral home to keep my mouth shut.

I well remember the moment I **saw** *his car leave the funeral home parking lot I* **had** *a very stupid and dangerous thought "I am now in charge!" I started strutting around the funeral home like I was the Archduke of Death, and I must have made myself look ridiculous. Well anyway, today I am embarrassed to even think about how I acted.*

In short order the widow of the decedent came to me and with tears running down her cheeks **asks** *me this question "Why do you think he did it?"*

I proceeded to tell her straight away why I thought he did it, and what I had to say back then on this sensitive subject – well it was a kid talking, it was insensitive, it was highly opinionated, it was unkind, and looking back it was totally unnecessary because in truth I wasn't in the least interested in exploring anything with her – hell, I didn't even know what exploring was, even though I had watched my employer doing it with her all afternoon. What is the saying? "Youth is wasted on the young." Well, in my case it sure was!

My employer's car pulled into the funeral home parking lot, and before he got into the building the widow had pulled him aside. I stood by the front door guiding my post, and knew by the look on his face and the blood draining from his lips, that I was in big, big trouble.

Around 8:00 p.m. that evening the widow left and my employer motioned for me to come to his office. I hated those moments in my life, but in truth I deserved most anything he was going to say to me. Instead of a scolding he looked at me and said this "Todd, you are terribly young. Next time just listen, and then walk with them, ask them questions, but keep your high level opinions to yourself. The funeral experience is a journey not a destination."

He was talking about taking the time and being sensitive to the process of exploring with another human being. He didn't even use the word "exploration" but that is precisely what he was talking about.

Possessing old-fashioned insights, approaches and ethics does not mean that a veteran funeral director cannot embrace the new memorial concepts like eternal reefs, or memory glass for instance, and likewise possessing youth does not automatically translate into high level creativity, and non-conformist risk taking. To say anything akin to this notion is just making a thoughtless sweeping comment about both groups of professionals which is just not true.

As time goes on in the development ***of your*** funeral interview approaches, you will perhaps discover a pattern, your own style; but this will only take shape because of the way you feel inside and hence, how you function, the way you are as a sensitive human being regardless of your age.

Discovering, examining, deciding what to keep and what to change in your own funeral interview exploring pattern, will provide the sort of professional and personal growth that I feel, will be most meaningful for you. Remember, we cannot change anything about our client families, we can only improve on our own skills and attitudes. Remember also that while books, seminars, writings, and speeches on the importance of exploring life issues with another human being are extremely helpful and valuable – the greatest value to help that any funeral professional has is what is in their hearts. This I believe is true for the simple reason that in the end all funeral service is a matter of the heart.

SOME PRACTICAL SUGGESTIONS.

Certain practical aspects of exploration in the funeral interview deserve careful consideration. I shall point out some of them, knowing that I can only touch briefly upon them. Again my wish is to stimulate a discussion and a dialogue – not to present pat answers but to help you find your own. Think about your responses to these questions.

- Did you help the bereaved family to come closer to a comfortable knowledge as to all their options and alternatives?

- Did you help the bereaved family explore and express what possibilities and creativities are open concerning designing a meaningful ceremony?
- Did you enable the client family to tell you how they genuinely feel, how things truly look to them?
- Did you let the client family explore what they wanted to do in their own way, or did you lead them in a direction you chose for them?
- Did your behavior truly indicate the absence of control and the presence of genuine exploration? Were they afraid to express themselves, and if so, what did you do to relieve this fear?
- Did you really want to listen to them, or did you want them to listen to you because you already had the answers to their problems, and because like I was 45 years ago you were anxious to "give them a piece of your mind," or worse yet because you really didn't want to hear more about their situations as you wouldn't have known what to do with it anyway?
- Are you prepared to let the client family take the initiative and you keep the exploring going as long as they need to?
- Are you skilled at quietly moving the funeral interview along with gentle persistence undetected by the client family?
- Are you prepared to let them assume final responsibility for themselves, or do we feel we must assume it for them?
- Are we prepared to explore with them by letting them lead, or do we need to have them follow us?

These are very tough questions to ask of ourselves, but they are also critical questions that when honestly confronted open the avenues for the continuous improvement of our funeral interview skills, particularly in the area of exploration. **Asking tough questions of oneself is one method of avoiding stale habits or worse acute burnout.**

Exploring with the client family means listening and gently responding to what they are saying and feeling. It means enabling them to express themselves fully and this can and does require genuine interest, and genuine positive regard.

In the funeral interview this means following them rather than asking them to follow us, while at the same time keeping the interview moving ahead.

The issue of control versus exploration in the funeral interview is of utmost importance in inspiring funeral professionals to move ahead and genuinely connect with the contemporary expectations of the modern consumer.

I feel it is very timely for funeral professionals who are actively engaged in the funeral interview experience to ponder seriously the thoughts expressed in the points made in the list of questions presented in this article.

There was a time when the funeral "director" was indeed the "the absolute director." I fear that some in our beloved profession still yearn and search for those times, I know I used to.

Sometimes, possibly many times, this still happens, but more and more the tension of who "leads" the funeral interviews becomes a gray area, a fuzzy area, not quite and clearly defined as it was some years ago. The solid skill *of* exploring, making new discoveries with a bereaved client family is a good safe way for funeral professionals to embrace change and move forward in service to humanity.

9. ENCOURAGEMENT

I hope that pretty much everything we do in the funeral interview we do to encourage the client family in one way or another by engaging them, by showing them kindness and attention. It has been my longtime observation that most, by far the vast majority of funeral professionals simply excel at showing clients, and basically the entire communities in which they work and live, kindness and attention. In such a complicated, impersonal and often times cynical world people who can show others kindness and attention are indeed sweet blessings!

Our attitude toward life, our approach to living, our responses as funeral professionals are all meant to support and reinforce the client family in their efforts to create memorial/ceremony decisions that are meaningful and worthwhile for them – we all know that.

We strive to assist them in coming closer to reality of death and to their own self-satisfaction with us and our company's services in order that they may experience the value and benefits of the entire memorial experience that we offer. In this ongoing effort, to create a meaningful experience, we cannot under estimate that our slightest "um-hum" is meant to spur them on in their selections, in their ceremony designing, and in their own personal establishment of an experience of value.

The "um-hum" while frowned upon by some thinkers I believe is an excellent interviewing skill to possess. The simple "um-hum" tells them this important psychological message: **"That's it. Go on. You're on your way. I'm with you. I care."**

This manner of encouraging our bereaved clients is an integral part of our professional funeral service philosophy. In fact, the "um-hum" almost becomes obligatory in helping other people, and you don't need a PhD either to use it effectively.

Like empathy, the "um-hum" is not really stated in words; it is more of a simple presence in us, and my personal experience is that like empathy the bereaved client family will sense it.

CASE STUDY: *When I was a student at the old New England Institute of Anatomy, Sanitary Science, Embalming and Funeral Directing in Boston, I worked alongside of one of the kindness, sweetest, and most outstanding funeral director I have ever encountered. His name was* **Alfred B. Marsh**, *and he was just a jewel in the crown of the human race.*

I did a great amount of Al's embalming as he was allergic to chemicals. I liked him so much, and admired him so much that I was continuously motivated to never ever disappoint him. I owe him a great deal of gratitude, and cherish his memory to this very day.

I remember I was helping Al work a visitation one evening. This lady came over to Al and she was a magpie, she just would not stop talking, she rambled almost randomly from one subject to another, she didn't even seem to need to breathe as it was clear that she never took a breath. Then on top of all this she was a bore.

I wasn't even in the conversation and I was so annoyed with her that I just turned around and stood staring at the front door. Now there is a very ineffective way to communicate or be nice to others - turning around and staring at the door.

Al couldn't get a word in edgewise. All he kept saying was "um-hum." I think he probably said "um-hum" five hundred times. I couldn't believe his tolerance and patience because obviously this talking machine who was dressed up like a human being was nuts!

Finally the ordeal ended. Al thanked her for the conversation, shook her hand, and walked quietly into the chapel. I was still standing staring at the front door, which really hadn't seen much action that particular night – that is kind of pitiful isn't it? A young man just staring at a front door of a funeral home that isn't being opened or closed for anyone.

The talking lady was ready to leave, and as she walked past me I said a silent prayer that she would not open up her mouth, but open it up she did, and she said to me "Your boss is a mighty smart man. He is such a gentleman, and it was so nice to talk with him and get his thoughts." Al had only said "um-hum" to this and that was it.

In short order here came Al, and he could probably see that the expression on my face betrayed my immature annoyance with this non-stop talking woman. I made some "crack" about how offensive this woman was, and Al, the consummate gentleman and funeral professional just smiled and said "Well, Todd you could look at it that way, but I just thought she was lonely and needed somebody to listen."

I felt might puny after that interaction with Al, but looking back it was precisely that depth of kindness and character that made Al so beloved and admired by so many people, and he really pulled it off by just muttering "um-hum.

10. AVOIDABLE PROBLEMS

Throughout my career I have worked hard to eliminate problems. Sounds utterly ridiculous doesn't it? A life without problems. What a utopian fantasy!

However in my early years in funeral service I was brain-washed, it was drummed into my thick head, and I was admonished over and over again that the worse crime which lay upon the face of the earth was making a mistake on a funeral. Problems on funerals were, in the philosophy of the veteran funeral directors who furnished me the "university" in my life, were intolerable, and if a problem arose it was grounds for severe consequences.

There was only one glaring problem with this ridged carved in stone attitude: the problem was that in reality problems abounded on funerals. In fact, looking back at my career I don't know, if truth be told, if I ever conducted a funeral where everything went precisely the way I planned it out. Probably if I didn't have to deal with other human beings, I mean if it were just myself and the decedent, then possibly everything would be to my liking – but I usually, most often, had to open the doors of the funeral home, cemetery or church, or temple and let people in. When people showed up the problems began.

Here is an example of problems people create. Have you ever given pall bearers instructions? Have you ever asked a group of pall bearers to "please face the hearse?" I concluded years ago that I would have a greater chance of success changing the financial structure of China than to get ALL the pall bearers to understand what face the hearse means let alone get them all to behave the way I wanted them to.

The example of the pall bearers is what I call an unavoidable mistake. It is an unavoidable problem, and it seems beyond anyone's ability to correct the state of the pall bearer's lack of listening ability.

Here would be another example: the family's personal car rear ending the funeral coach. I had this happen. The family had decided to drive their own car, which was following the hearse. I put the brake on, and I looked into the side mirror and had that horrible feeling of knowing I was going to be hit, and there was nothing I could do to avoid the collision. This is another instance of an unavoidable problem.

The family member driving the car hit the hearse so hard that the back door was smashed in to such an extent we couldn't get the decedent out to complete the burial service. We had to go to the auto body shop to get the back door taken off. You can just imagine how thrilled the chaps that worked in the auto body shop were when first they saw me roll in, and second when they discovered that yes indeed there was a dead person in the back! That door came off in record time!

With all this said, I would like to suggest that there are also **AVOIDABLE PROBLEMS** which with a little awareness and attention can be within the control of the funeral professional to insure that they will not happen.

Here is an example which receives little if any attention but which I believe is worthy of exploring: **external conditions in the funeral home that can and should be avoided include interruptions and interferences.**

About these two I feel rather strongly. The funeral conference interview is a basically demanding experience of all the participants and so focus, privacy, and protection of this experience are very critical.

Here is an example. I worked in the management of a funeral home where a particular funeral arranger was employed who was just weak in their skills. This person was not weak in manners, nor in information taking, their weaknesses where primarily centered in their annoying addiction to creating interruptions on their own and tolerating interferences from others.

I sat in on several conferences that this funeral director was responsible for and in one three hour session this person jumped up and left and room, returned, and then jumped up again – now get this: 20 times!

On top of this annoying behavior, this funeral director had instructed the outer lobby receptionist to alert her to any and all phone calls, even if they were calls which had nothing to do with the matters presently at hand.

Not surprisingly this funeral director received so many negative family surveys that in time their employment was terminated.

Looking back at this situation, and after having scores of conversations with this person, after writing this person up countless times, in the end nothing changed. The pitiful part of this was that changing the approach to the arrangement interview in which interferences, and interruptions would have not been tolerated would have been so easy, and the management of the firm would have supported this policy 100%.

Why then do you think this funeral director not only tolerated such intrusions, but actually participated in them and encouraged them? Why would any adult, mature funeral professional behave in such a manner?

I concluded that this funeral director was so insecure, so fragile, so needy that they actually interpreted jumping up and down, leaving the office, returning, and then adding that messages came in from the outside on a regular basis, that in a very unhealthy way this activity, these annoying interferences and constant interruptions in the end made this funeral director the center of the universe in the arrangement conference, not the clients.

The funeral/cemetery interview demands, among other things, that the serving person concentrate as completely as possible on the present situation, thus establishing rapport and building trust. Jumping up and down, leaving the room and accepting messages that have nothing to do with the needs of the clients never will create an atmosphere of rapport and trust. Never!

Outside interruptions, even rare ones, no matter their perceived legitimacy can only hinder the important goals of building trust and establishing rapport. I have long thought that the typical funeral/cemetery professional has a window of time of about 10 minutes to establish trust and respect. Friends, this is not very long!

Priest, rabbi's, ministers, have years to accomplish this. Hospice nurses have weeks and months, but funeral professionals have a terribly limited span of time to establish trust and respect. It is to the credit of most in our profession that interruptions and interferences are either eliminated altogether, or kept at an essential minimum, and only allowed in the instance of a global threat to the world!

Phone calls, knocks on the door, well-meaning people who want "just a word" with you, secretaries who must have you sign this document "at once," or the Gross National Product will collapse, may well destroy in seconds what you and the client family have tried hard to build.

In my humble opinion I believe one of the key substances of the funeral interview is that it is simply sacred; such as the sacred relationship between a physician, attorney or a religious cleric. The funeral interview is also extremely personal and deserves and needs respect for both confidentiality and privacy.

I have actually seen some gutsy and creative funeral professionals make a practice of putting on the door a sign reading "Do Not Disturb" or something similar, and they mean it! Although this practice might be helpful, I feel it could also possibly have the opposite affect and frighten and/or intimidate the client family waiting outside or, at least, make them feel more anxious than they already are.

Another totally avoidable interference and interruption is when the funeral professional is themselves so disorganized, so disjointed, so discombobulated, so rattled, and so unprofessional that the funeral interview is cut off and then started up again numerous times because of the incompetency of the funeral/cemetery counselor.

When you have a bumbling incompetent, licensed or not, behaving this way when they are confronted with their counterproductive approach usually endless excuses are usually provided. These unfortunate people try valiantly to spin their incompetency into magnanimous altruistic behaviors by retreating into the parrot- like intonation that they were checking: checking with a good heart, checking to make sure everything was ship shape, checking on the newspapers, checking on the vault, checking on the flowers, checking on the death certificate, checking, checking, checking and then more checking.

To be sure there are times in which we must leave the room, but 5, 6, 7, 8, 9 or 20 times in one funeral/cemetery interview is pressing the limits of the common sense approach to this sacred experience.

Funeral/cemetery professionals who are well prepared, highly interested in their performance, who have their client families absolute best interests at heart, who are secure and grounded in who they are as human beings, and who have successfully established trust and respect with the client family, do not behave in such a manner.

Disorganized, disjointed, discombobulated, rattled and frazzled funeral/cemetery interviews are never the fault of the client family, never ever. This is always the glaring fault of the funeral professional interviewing the client family and the good news is situation is totally avoidable.

11. TIME

The American culture measures much of what we do in terms of time and we set a great deal of value on time as to whether we fail or succeed.

Our cultural slang, jargon is resplendent with old sayings concerning time. Have you ever heard this? "A stitch in time saves nine," (whatever that means?) or "Time waits for no one," or "Time is money." Therefore, time, how it is used and or abused, is an important factor in the funeral interview because time is important to people. These days "quick time" "fast time" are ingrained in the American psyche. If a fast meal at McDonald's takes too long people get impatient, annoyed, angry, and some people simply march out and go somewhere else.

Now I am not in the least suggesting that ordering a Number 3 at McDonald's is on the same level as being involved with a death situation, but at the same time (pardon the pun) I am saying that people will care for their dead in a consistent manner with how they live their lives. If people expect fast food in fast time, and they have lived with this expectation for years, the probability is high that they will march right into the funeral/cemetery office with the same expectation.

The central subject here is time. So let us begin by asking an important question concerning our professional work and our attitude towards time – and particularly our client's time, not just ours.

When we schedule a funeral interview for ten in the morning, are we there and actually available in person to the client family at ten in the morning?

This may strike some as a strange place to begin, but I have seen some terribly disorganized funeral operations that even this minimal responsibility becomes the impossible dream.

Promptness and organized schedules is more than merely a matter of courtesy. The longer bereaved clients (or any clients for that matter) are kept waiting the more they can easily start to wonder (most times in silence) what else will be mishandled? They might silently be thinking whether they are of no importance to us? Or whether we are keeping them waiting intentionally for some dark ulterior purpose unknown to them (changing prices or something worse)? Or whether we are being or will even be fair with them since by our actions of not being ready to meet them and help has already set the stage for mistrust.

Every experienced funeral director or cemeterian knows full well that many times what the client family's imaginations can whip up about us is amazingly unreal, but the important point to remember is that no matter how unfounded or exaggerated, their thoughts are as real to the person who imagined it!

You get the point. They might already be suspicious of us, so why add to this an already risky situation by being late or tardy for the set appointment time?

What this means in terms of client trust and respect concerning us is obvious. Appointments should be kept on time or at the very least a very good and sufficient reason should be given or an honest explanation as to what happened, and we don't need to include any "shop" talk in our explanation either. Here is an example of what not to do: "Oh, I am sorry I am running late, we just got back from a house call, and you know how slow the police are in situations like this."

If your desired result is to unleash your client's wild imagination on the loose just use this type of explanation as to why you are tardy, and you will succeed beyond your wildest hopes and dreams. Your explanations should be like the old woman's dance, short and sweet. Something possibly like this, "My apologies to you, I was unavoidably delayed, and I do hope you will forgive me."

I feel it wise to never use phony and feeble excuses like we have all experienced in places like the pharmacy, the auto mechanic, the dry cleaner and yes, even in the hospital.

There are few, if any experienced funeral directors, who have not experienced the following. Someone had died at a hospital and mysteriously the head nurse or the security guard in truth just simply forgets to call the funeral home about the death. At 9:00 a.m. the next morning, the bereaved family walks in and announces they are in our establishment to make arrangements for a decedent which we –don't know anything about.

After an internal investigation the error is finally uncovered, a phone call is made from the funeral home to the hospital, and inevitably the nurse or the security guard once again offers the well-used, worn out, utterly predictable and terribly feeble excuse "Well, the shift was changing, that's what happened." I actually used to believe that excuse, until a veteran funeral professional set me straight.

Time can be abused in other ways. For instance, we all have had this happen. Someone rushes into the funeral home/cemetery unannounced, without any prior appointment and insists on seeing you at once.

This can be a sticky wicket because many times there is no compelling reason to or sometimes even beyond our ability to drop everything and see them. I have concluded many years ago that the death of another human being can indeed create a crisis, but I have discovered that what is a crisis to a client should not toss the funeral home/cemetery into a crisis. I am not talking about a death emergency where it is a house call, a police/coroner call or the like. These instances require immediate attention, and certainly our traditional "walk-in" clients must be served, but they also must understand patience if their announced presence risks putting the schedule of the funeral home/cemetery in jeopardy.

I know this sounds harsh but I have seen many funeral operations thrown into absolute bedlam because some person "walked in" and demanded to see a funeral professional when none was available. **The operative word here is DEMAND!**

I believe we need to re-evaluate our historic stance that ALL death situations are in reality, dramatic emergencies which compare to a building burning down with people still in the building. I believe this historic approach to death in a mortuary is overstated and overdone. To be sure it is understandable that most any person would be upset, nervous, grieved, and sad when they need our attention, but no funeral interview takes that long, **OR SHOULD TAKE THAT LONG**, that a "walk in" cannot be tended to in a reasonable time frame. What is not necessary is the ancient theatrical reaction that if someone does not get up on the floor "a.s.a.p." disaster is waiting for the funeral home around the corner.

Professional activities (even hospital emergency rooms and veterinarians) function on schedules and appointments. When no appointment was made, and if you are serving another client or on a service, or have an already scheduled appointment, then you are legitimately occupied. If the client family must see you that day then they will have to wait until you are free or make an appointment so see someone else, or set up a scheduled appointment at a set hour and day to see you.

This is not a policy that is uncaring, for on the contrary were you to see this family when preoccupied with other client concerns, or the very worse try to see them both simultaneously (see **CASE STUDY**), you would be so distracted and tense to listen to either of them in the way you would like. There are always exceptions to this, but honesty has a way of smoothing out relationships. It is the honest helping procedure to do everything we can to set up appointments, and stick to them, and if we cannot see a walk-in or random appointment without taking away from other set appointments, we need to be firm but gentle that a set appointment needs to be made.

CASE STUDY: *It is a liberating feeling to admit to the reader that I have made every mistake in the funeral book. It is true, but through it all my love of our beloved profession has kept me going. It is love that makes all the difference in the world. Part of my love of funeral service is my memories of the extremely interesting funeral professionals who I worked with in the infancy of my career. I mentioned in the last paragraph the high risk activities of* trying to serve two family clients simultaneously, you know the funeral director who wants to do it all.

I bring this up because I actually saw one funeral director attempt this (serving two families at once). I believe to this day that he thought it would work, but in the end it was a colossal flop.

Oh, here is a footnote. This funeral professional was the poster boy for the self-obsessed egotist. He was a modern day "Narcissus." Because of his addiction to his own self-absorption he actually thought that he could say whatever he wanted to anybody (except, of course, the boss). He also thought that any death call required a response time which would compare with our ambulance calls, complete with high speed, siren and lights.

For instance, the coroner's office would call and give us a first call on the death of an unknown, homeless person who had been in the morgue for a month and this chap would fly into overdrive action. I was young, but even back then I thought he was a "nut."

One day a scheduled family arrived, and in they went with this particular funeral director to make their arrangements. About ten minutes later a second family just walked in coming directly from the hospital where their father had died. As I was explaining to the second family that the funeral professional was engaged (which they totally understood) my agitated egoist associate came flying out of the office, saw the second family, froze in his tracks, and then plunged and bungled into our conversation and told them that he would wait on them immediately.

He took them into a second office, and then the funeral arrangement acrobatics began.

In fact, the funeral home staff just stood in the foyer of the mortuary watching him run from office to office like a lunatic. One staff member actually had a stop watch on his wrist watch and kept time. This odd and strange scrambling funeral director got through it, but the truth is both families felt rushed, and one even complained. I thought both could have complained.

Even when confronted with the client complaint, this funeral director refused to admit that he had done a foolish and reckless thing by trying to show off in front of the people he worked with by being totally insensitive and totally disorganized about his own use of his professional time.

Our awareness, our respect, and our sensitivities to time is very important, and in our fast paced life, which seems to laugh at time sensitivities, I would humbly suggest that this issue is today all the more magnified in a profession such as funeral and cemetery service.

Setting interview times, and moving the funeral interview on with gentle persistence has wisdom and will help solve a myriad of potential difficulties. Sometimes boundaries must be clearly drawn, because some people go on talking without realizing they are repeating themselves. Some clients honestly may not know how to end the interview, and then get up and leave. Being products of our society, they may feel that the polite thing to do is to sit and await a signal from the funeral professional that the funeral interview is actually over.

I do not mean that we should ever rush the client family, but I do mean that we should make clear to them the time available so that they can orient themselves within it. I have no precise answer as to how long an interview should be but as one veteran funeral director said to me many years ago two considerations concerning interviewing time need to be at least considered 1) we are not wasting the family client's time, and 2) the funeral interview has to come to an end sometime.

One final practical point: if you must and are compelled to interview several client families in one day, always allow a few minutes between funeral interviews to write or fill in your notes, to think over what has just gone on, or just to relax and get ready for the next family. Otherwise you may, like I have done many times, in your mind, keep on talking to family "*A*" while family "**B**" is sitting there. Family "**B**" is entitled to your full attention.

Get family "A" off your mind before seeing family "B". To do this you may well need a few minutes to mull things over, note on your work sheet what you promised family "**A**" you would look into, or just sit back or walk around the funeral home once to get ready for family "**B**".

Try it. It works.

12. SILENCE

Every day we hear many people talking. In fact, it seems a safe observation to assert that talking people, nonstop talking people are literally everywhere. They talk every minute of every hour and they never stop!

Nonstop talking people, if a person stops talking long enough to think this out, is a new phenomenon in life. Never before in pre-literate or literate society has it been possible for human beings to talk constantly, everywhere with no end.

Because of this cultural state of our addiction to talking, bringing up the value of silence might strike many as odd and strange. What can a human being possibly find valuable in silence, and how in the world does this apply to our profession?

There are many kinds of silences. Given our current penchant to engage in constant talking, silences usually make people uncomfortable and hence, their discomfort is corrected or eliminated by talking, whether they have something to say or not.

Here is an example of being uncomfortable with silence. My experience has been that most beginning (newly licensed) funeral/cemetery interviewers find silence difficult to bear, if not downright intolerable. They innocently seem to think that if it occurs, they are at fault and the lapse should be remedied at once. They ought to be saying something, and something profound!

They regard silence as a breach of professional etiquette that must be corrected on the spot. Motivated as they are, because they don't want to feel uncomfortable, they many times end up sometimes talking too much. I know this happened to me in my early years. In time most funeral interviewers learn to differentiate between silences, to appreciate and react to them differently, but this is an acquired skill, and unfortunately some don't ever get it.

There are, as mentioned before, different kinds of silence. For example, there is the silence of a client family member that may require additional silence from us to help them and we also sort out thoughts and feelings. **Respect, understanding and tolerance for this silence is more beneficial than any words from the funeral/cemetery professional.** Should the silence endure, we may want to interject a brief remark to help this person go on. People can get lost in silence and will actually appreciate this gesture on our part as being a good indication of a possible way out and also that we were paying close attention.

Occasionally a silence arises, the cause of which is quite clear to the funeral professional. The client family may have related something so heartwarming, so tragic, so shocking or so frightening, that both partners feel the need to absorb it to the depths in mutual silence – and this is indeed the appropriate thing to do. If after such a silence if the client family still finds it difficult to continue, a comment such as, "It must have been a heartwarming experience for you" or "I don't know what to say, I am so terribly sorry" will often help them pick up the threads again.

Another cause of silence is confusion. A given situation may be confusing to the client family. This can easily happen in our profession. We contend with endless forms, numbers and more numbers, new people, new places, deadline notifications, difficult decisions; truth is no matter how easy we intend to make it, the funeral interview can be a daunting experience. Here, the shorter the silence the better, lest confusion compound confusion. You, as the funeral/cemetery professional, will have to act to alleviate the tension in a manner appropriate to the situation and to your own appraisal of it.

Here are some thoughts which you might find helpful. For instance, "What I said just now about the certified copies of the death certificate seems to have caused confusion." This alone may be sufficient; if not, you might add, "What I meant was…" and then rephrase your statement. Most likely this will elicit a response. The sure approach is that confused silence on the part of the client family requires immediate action on the part of the funeral professional.

The silence of a client resistance is something else again. The client family may be silent because they are resisting what they consider to be intrusive probing or perceived or real pressuring on our parts. Some client families may see in you and I an authority figure to be opposed or avoided (most funeral professionals have certainly encountered this). The funeral professional may well find this type of silence the hardest to deal with because he or she may tend to feel rejected, opposed, and thwarted. If the funeral/cemetery director is addicted to being accepted, well-liked and popular with every single human being on earth this type of silence can be torture.

CASE STUDY: *For several years in my career I was employed by a wonderful funeral director named John B. Turner from Cedar Rapids, Iowa. John and I became good friends, and I have cherished his memory over the long veil of time. We served approximately 800 families a year. Because of the number of services, we took as a matter of course, as an ingrained habit, of doing arrangements the "Turner way" which meant taking vital statistics, setting up service times, and selling merchandise; you know the old A, B, C's of making funeral arrangements. One day I went into the office to start making arrangements with a family, I remember 5 people were sitting in the room. I sat down, did my standard preliminaries and started on the vital statistics. "What was your mother's full name?" I asked. Dead silence. The 5 people simply stared off into space. I silently thought, "Well, here we go once again." I told them that this might have been a difficult question (their mother's name!), and we would come back to it later. I then asked "When was your mother born?" Again they said nothing absolute silence. My next thought was "You are in a pickle, Todd!" I had no clue what to do except to just wing it, and make it up as I went – this was not covered in Mortuary College.*

Making it up as I went I said, "I can see that there is a problem. If you wish I can leave the room and you can talk it out in private, or you can come back later, or you can share your issue with me, or I can ask another funeral director to come in and serve you."

In my wildest dreams I never thought they would take me up on my last option about getting another funeral director, but that is just what they did. For some reason they did not like Todd Van Beck (unbelievable, I know). Their rejection of me almost made me throw up. I was sick about it for days, and the other funeral director who ended up serving them used to walk by me and whisper "They liked me better than you" which was absolutely true! As much as his ribbing stung it was the gospel truth.

The critical point of this case study is that their silence was indeed a clear message directed at me and I missed it by being too concerned with getting done what I wanted done. I learned some tremendous lessons from this type of silence and some of the lessons were: I had better use open-ended questions and focus on trust and rapport before I do anything else, I cannot be all things to all people, and if as a funeral professional I am addicted, yes addicted, to be well liked and popular I have already sealed the certainty of my failure with many people by possessing this immature attitude. I simply cannot be all things to all people no matter how good I thought I was.

Of course, as all funeral directors already know there are no quick answers to this, save for emphasizing our beginning comments concerning the urgent issue of needing to establish trust and respect with a client or client family quickly, and asking them immediately what is pressing on their minds. This approach seems to be a safe and sensible way to proceed with our valued clients.

Finally, there are the brief silences, the short pauses, during which the client family may simply be searching for more thoughts and feelings to express.

Therefore, it is best not to rush, not to interpret a short silence as a command from above for us to swing into action, but to quietly wait and be prepared for what will come. Usually something will follow these short "thinking silences" from the client family. What it will be only God knows, but usually something will be forthcoming.

I have arrived at the thought that it is these brief silences that make the funeral/cemetery conference so terribly interesting, because we never know exactly what is going to pop out of our client's mouths. I personally find this the great unknown challenge in working with bereaved clients. We just never know what is going to happen!

Inevitably both the client family and the funeral professional will sometimes speak at the same moment and both then retreat with apologies and encouragements to the other to continue. This can be awkward, and a bit of humor (be very careful with humor) may assist us. I am assuming, of course, that we are interested in listening to the client family and do not feel that we must have our say just then and in everything later on. We can interject a short remark "I'm sorry, go ahead." Frequently just a smile with an encouraging nod will be sufficient. Or, "I was just wondering aloud what you were thinking about?"

What is interesting to me is that most every religious movement in the long eventful history of the human experience has placed a tremendous value on silence. In fact, some religious teachings very seriously instruct that if there is too much babbling, too much chatter, too much interference the ability to spiritually connect with the divine is severely limited.

It seems to me that in so many death situations people, even people who have spent a lifetime asserting that they have no need to connect to any spirit, turn to silence in order to make that connection. In many life experience silence serves as our spiritual bridge in life and death situations.

We live in a world of clatter. We live in a world where the clanging gong is nonstop. We live in a world where we actually are spellbound by talking heads who wear cosmetics, and are reading prepared scripts.

With all this however, there still exits the world of the cemetery, the world of the mortuary, a world that is not as visible as it once was to be sure, but nonetheless still a presence. Our world confronts life, but also honestly confronts death, its reality, and its consequences. Silence certainly does have a valuable position as being one of the landmark skills for any funeral professional in our vocation.

13. PERSONAL EXAMPLES CAN HINDER

My experience in the use of personal examples (from my funeral service career) is that such memories which hold great meaning for me might not hold that much meaning for others, so I have concluded that as tempting as this activity might be it ought to be used cautiously.

Personal example's from a funeral career is not the same thing as relying on experiential expertise as a professional internal navigator and guide. For instance, I have had some of the most hilarious things happen on death calls, funeral, burials and cremation, but if I would share those personal examples, probably the clients would faint dead away!

It seems a safe way to go that if we are not convinced that it will helpful for the client family (our personal story), a safe rule is to be conservative with career history storytelling (and to be sure funeral directors do like to tell stories, myself included).

Now, if the client family solicits these experiences the situation is thereby changed, and we may well choose to comply with this request. But even then it is prudent to qualify words with a remark such as "This has worked for others, but I can't say whether it will work for you" or "This helped other clients, but I wonder how you feel about it as regards to yourself." In this way, we indicate that it is the client family who is central in the situation and that they need not copy my example or anyone else's examples. The client family will also realize that we do not look upon our experience or examples as necessarily providing the solution for them.

One approach which is less confronting is to draw upon the experiences of others by means of distant generalizations and depersonalizations. For example: "I have known clients who when faced with a similar situation have found it helpful to . . . . . How do you feel about this?" or "People do come up against problems like this. They often feel better when they are able to . . . . How does this strike you?" There still remains the danger that the client family will think they ought to adopt the course mentioned because others have and particularly because we have pointed this out, but I have discovered this is only a minimal danger.

One great skill which contemporary funeral/cemetery professions have embraced and I believe excelled at, is making suggestions. Let's explore this a moment.

A suggestion is a mild form of advice. **It is offering an idea that another person has not thought of before.** Its overtones tend to be tentative and vague. In it the funeral professional proffers possible lines of actions. A suggestion does not demand compliance nor threaten the client family with consequences should they decide not follow it through. I am speaking of true suggestions, and not of masked commands.

Suggestions provides the client family with the funeral professionals considered opinions but leaves them free leeway to accept, refuse, or propose ideas of their own. Indeed its purpose may be to stimulate the client family to think and plan for themselves. When this is the funeral professional's sincere intention, a suggestion communicates this silent thought: **I think my suggestion is a good one and may work. It's up to you, of course, to decide.** If clearly stated as a suggestion and genuinely intended as such, it is an open form of communication rather than closed, it is provisional rather than final.

It is equal speaking to equal, by one of whom hopefully may possess more information, knowledge, or experience, as most funeral professionals possess, but is not determined to force it on the other. I firmly believe at the beginning of the 21st century funeral/cemetery professionals must absolutely include the professional's ability, skill and interest in taking on a new job: that of the suggestion maker.

The more suggestions the better!

Finally, concerning suggestions, two items loiter in the background of too many funeral interviews and need to be put to rest. The first is, "If I were you, I would. . ." The client family's reaction may well be "Well, I just don't believe it. If you were me, you'd feel just as confused and unsure as I do, and so there would be two of us, neither knowing what to do."   "If you were me, you wouldn't say that!" "If you were me, you wouldn't know what to do any more than I do!"

The second point concerning suggestions needs only a coup de grace in funeral service. His name is **"I know just how you feel and I did . . . ."** The client family thinks: "I'm not taken in. How can you 'know' how I 'feel?' Is your child also dead right now? And if you do know, so what" You don't feel the way I feel or you would never think of saying that you know." This funeral interview suggestion approach is very cold and very remote. If a funeral interviewer saying such a thing has a mind, then they surely have no heart, and so away with them is my vote.

What I do believe is that the funeral professional must gently and quietly lead and question and make wise and valid suggestions to such an extent that the role of the client family is positively affected as the experience of their loss and hopefully in the end, expresses itself in meaning, but what is meaningful for them – not us.

However, I have no mixed feelings about the following attempt at encouragement in the funeral interview. The funeral professional should avoid it like the plague. Here are several examples of the interview plague: "Well, you know, everyone has to go through this sooner or later." "Every cloud has its silver lining, and by tomorrow morning you'll feel much better." "A good night's sleep always helps, so why don't you try that?" As ridiculous as these responses sound they nonetheless have been used in funeral interviews in the past. This type of encouragement expressed to a client family is in the end belittling to the professionalism which is expected from all funeral professionals.

If we genuinely feel with the client family what he or she is feeling, if we can let them know by our behavior that we are feeling with them and interested in them just as hard as we can, and if we are able to show this without getting in their way, we shall not need to tell them, for they will already know. They will understand that we shall never know just exactly how and what they feel but that as another human being we are trying our best and showing them that we are trying.

14. COMMON SENSE

Phases, divisions, or stages in the funeral interview always indicate movement in the interview and also indicates that you are watching yourself as the funeral professional and not getting stuck. If movement in the funeral interview is absent, this may indicate that we are indeed stuck. Then there is no movement forward at all and can actually be a waste of our client family's time.

On the other hand, movement may be so swift that it is very difficult to determine just where one stage ends and the next one begins, and this is not good either.

Balance here is the watchword. I would like to suggest that the three stages of the funeral interview are: Initiation, Exploration and Closing.

I would like to make clear that I am not telling other funeral professionals how to proceed with a funeral interview per se; I am devoted to exploring the nuances of the interview, not presenting a how-to guide. Most all funeral professionals are well versed in the techniques of the funeral interview, but once in a while taking time to review and think about what we are doing is always a good idea, it seems to me.

In the initial stage of the funeral interview the matter about why the funeral professional and client family are meeting should be stated. Interestingly, I have discovered that some family clients are so confused, so grieved, and so distracted that they don't know precisely why they are with us, nor do they know that they want, or what to expect.

The initial phase generally centers about the decisions that the client family needs to address concerning the death of another human being, the practical decisions concerning the legal disposition of a decedent, and ceremonial creativity. In actuality however, the initiation of the funeral interview may not deal exclusively or even primarily with these matters. Historically these matters have been on the agenda of most funeral professionals, but in today's world of customer/client skepticisms, cynicisms, and trust issues and a myriad of other unknown and unexpected points may easily arise, and what seemed so central to us at first may diminish in importance and be replaced by another subjects of importance to the client family from God knows where. This possibility is particularly relevant to the process of the funeral professional's interview in contemporary times. **In other words, in these turbulent days in the funeral world anything can happen.**

Here are some common sense ideas concerning our subject which I hope the reader will find helpful, because in the end, is that not the ethical goal behind all funeral interviews – the noble goal of simply being helpful to another human being.

Implementing honest listening and sincere absorbing of what we have just heard are key internal conditions that logically follow each other in the substance of the funeral interview: being honest with ourselves so that we may be honest with our clients.

Beginning funeral interviewers are often so concerned with just getting the basic required essential details correct, trying to simply understand all that is going on, and just getting through the funeral interview that they miss the fact that they have not connected with the client family.

I know this vulnerability in confidence in making funeral arrangements certainly happened to me when I started out, and truth is sometimes it still does – there are no guarantees in the funeral interview process.

This is understandable, we have all been there and that is easy enough to understand, but this interviewing awkwardness, in the end is not beneficial to anyone if it continues. What is called for in a good old-fashioned dose of humility? Humility most always redirects the focus from us to others, and this is a tremendous asset in creating a meaningful funeral interview.

Gentle humility with us and others is a highly valued skill in the funeral interview. Humility is also a sign of inner maturity that takes time to develop; perhaps <u>a good starting point is to realize, with genuine humility, is that what we say is generally much less important than we think it is.</u>

When we start out in the beginning stages of our careers in the funeral interview we may be so insecure and so enthusiastic that our own eagerness gets in the way and we miss the asset of being humble entirely. Prideful enthusiasm can be fatal in trying to help people.

We also, in reality, may be so unsure of ourselves that we feel the need to prove how confident and important we are, and once again humility just vanishes.

Looking back at my own beginning work in funeral decision making, I know I made many embarrassing and foolish mistakes, and even today I know of no remedy for this except patience and awareness of ourselves constantly looking inward to locate, lock on, and then hold on to the mature substance which marks the quality of the successful funeral interview.

No matter our lack of humility or how annoyingly insecure or immature we might be, we can take heart for no matter what I have discovered, most times to my own chagrin and embarrassment: **the client family will usually set us straight – if we only let them.**

The interview in the funeral service profession is more a developed art and skill than it is a science and for this reason alone it is difficult to teach. Every artist must discover his or her own style and the tools with which he or she works best; and so it is with our quest for substance and meaning of the funeral interview. Style matures with experience, stimulation, and reflection. I am not interested in you adopting my style, but I am very much interested in stimulating you to develop and reflect upon your own style. There is no magic dust or magic potion, but there is interestingly one single magic bullet – and that single magic bullet in our beloved profession is YOU – YOU the funeral professional.

Once the initiation formalities of greeting and being seated are over, the most useful thing we can do to get started is to ask the all-important open ended question: "Do you have anything that you would like to talk about before we begin?" Then listen just as hard as possible to what the family has to say. If we feel we must say something, it ought to be brief and neutral, for we do not wish to get in the client's way: "Please tell me what has happened?" or "Please feel free to tell me what's on your mind." (These short phrases are not scripts, only brief suggestions.)

Sometimes at the outset of the funeral interview, there is room or need for small talk on the funeral professional's part, something to help the family get started, but we should attempt this only when we truly feel that it will be helpful. Brief statements such as the following may break the ice: "With traffic the way it is today did you have difficulty in traveling?" or "We had a pretty mild winter this year." Remember however that **small talk is just that, small in meaning and importance.**

By ignoring the brief and neutral open ended question as a beginning "Do you have anything on your mind right now?" the funeral interview can easily start off on a different note when the funeral professional jumps in too quickly and is the one who has initiated inadvertently the direction of the interview.

The great danger in these funeral professional-initiated interviews is the possibility that they will turn into monologues or lectures by the funeral professional or worse, a combination of the two. We can avoid this danger if we are humbly careful to stop after we have asked that all important beginning open ended question. Then we can furnish the information and the interview gently moves forward.

At this point we need to, with gentle persistence, move forward with the task of the funeral interview that being: 1) decisions concerning the disposition of the decedent, 2) decisions, designs, and development of ceremonial services and activities including the memorial product goods and services which accompany such ceremonial decisions and investment considerations of financial concerns.

If we want to have a general conversation of good communication, we shall see to it that the client family has this opportunity to express themselves fully after the important tasks of the funeral interview have been completed. I have discovered over the years that there is such a thing and such a distinct possibility of the funeral interview taking so long, and the funeral professional being so long winded that in the end the bereaved client families' time has been truly abused.

Common sense points concerning the funeral interview:

- Assist the individual and/or client family to make their own decisions.
- Involve themselves with more than the solution to an immediate problem.
- Concern themselves with attitudes rather than with simply decisions.
- Recognize and respect that the helping interview involves emotions rather than purely intellectual attitudes.
- Perceive that the helping interview involves establishing a quick rapport of trust relationships between people.

15. AUTHORITY

The issue on the table is how funeral/cemetery professionals apply authority in helping clients and to what end.

If as funeral/cemetery professionals we use our licensed authority as a defense and barricade while the funeral interview and experience is proceeding, are we indicating, implying, or stating: "This or that is not to be discussed," "That is a professional secret," "You'll just have to take my word for it," "I know best," "This is final; there is nothing to add"?

When the client family is confronted with such attitudes particularly in our present time, it is not surprising if they feel that they are being hemmed in and treated like an object. They may well submit, as they certainly did in years gone by in our profession, but in the 21st century I see that they rebel and sometimes kick back by surfing the internet for answers and options in front of us.

CASE STUDY: *This will be a short case study. I am thinking that many of the veteran funeral directors reading this may well relate to the following. When I started my career I worked for a dictator funeral director. He told people where to sit, when to stand, and he even told priests following a Funeral Mass if he thought they had talked to long during their* *homily.* I *was terrified of him.*

Looking back however, is the glaring fact that he was very successful in being a great American funeral director. People liked him very much and admired and respected him even more. We had no cremation – none. His funerals were cookie cutter funerals – literally the same repeat time after time after time.

The difference is not necessarily the makeup and character of my first boss, because I will make a statement that I suspect there are still "dictator" funeral directors out in the great big world.

The difference is that the culture changed. My first employer died just as the "consumer" movement was beginning in this country. No one ever price shopped our firm, no one ever questioned his directions, and trust me folks, he directed people. Looking back his approach of "I know what's best for you" actually worked.

Of course anyone reading this knows those days are long and forever gone! What about authority in the 21st century then? Here are some random thoughts. If as a funeral/cemetery professional, you tend to talk as much or talk even more than the client family, chances are good that you are blocking communication from them to you by asserting artificial authority.

It is quite likely that you are acting as an authority, as the superior in the funeral interview who must be respectfully listened to, and that you wish for the client family to perceive you in this way. **The problem is that these days' people are not looking for dictatorial authority - they are looking for dedicated relationships.**

Do we tend to let the client family finish what they have to say, or do we often finish it for them and then turn around and reply to our own response? Do we tend to interrupt the client family because we feel confident that we are so bright and quick that we can actually catch their intent, read their minds so to speak, and then become impatient if they keep on talking, because we have already GOT IT? Believing that we have heard "this kind of funeral stuff" many times in the past and then do we become bored and cut them off? Or do we see ourselves as an extremely experienced funeral professional that has developed the enviable skill of magical telepathy and mind reading? These are mighty difficult questions. My prediction is that most readers already have certain people popping into their minds.

Interruptions which are stimulated by the funeral directors authority complex creates a major communication obstacle in the funeral interview moving forward with grace and dignity. It cuts short vital and important communication that should actually be taking place. Most funeral professionals who interrupt constantly usually confess with great sincerity that their motives are all for the best, but in the helping process it can be seen as an abuse of authority. To show our client families that we understand them so well that we can finish their sentences is truly an abuse of our authority. Altruistic motives notwithstanding, in reality, when we are interrupting we are actually choking off what is coming our way, although we may sincerely believe ourselves to be helping the conversation based on a misguided notion of imagined authority that we have been given by possessing this or that certificate which hangs on the wall.

CASE OF THE ABUSE OF AUTHORITY – THE PREOCCUPATION WITH SELF

Have you ever been introduced to any funeral directors who you concluded after the introductions had great big egos? If you can answer this question in the affirmative, this portion of the writing ought to be of interest.

A basic factor in funeral communication relates more to the funeral professional's behavior than to the client family. As the funeral interview proceeds, you, the funeral professional, may be asking yourself what to say or do next. This concern with your own role may so absorb your attention that you will not be genuinely listening to the client family. You will be preoccupied with that small voice inside that insists on knowing how to act next. This inner voice constitutes a clear authoritarian obstacle to communication. This is not to be confused with the other inner voice that brings you closer to the world of the client family – that "third ear" with which you suddenly understand something haltingly expressed from the client family.

This is the voice of authority that insists on knowing what to do next and is in truth a block between you and client family, and being more concerned with the impression of authority you will make on them than with the impressions they might make on you if you were listening and trying to understand them.

Another Authority Pitfall: The Issue of Questions

Let us examine the absurdities of the endless overloading of questions. I am referring to what is known as "bombarding" with questions. Here, the helping tool of using endless questions becomes a weapon based on authority wielded in reality against the client family, if not in a deadly manner, then at least in one that can hardly inspire trust, make for rapport, or create an atmosphere in which the partners in the funeral interview finds themselves safe, secure and tended to by a person of kind sensitivity. The use of unbridled authority can easily create the environment which is the opposite of security and safety, and instead creates an environment where people are caught in a hailstorm of questions; and if the client family runs (escapes) to the nearest shelter (like the funeral home parking lot or restroom facilities), we can only admire their urge to survive.

Authority, dictatorial behaviors rarely do well in the helping experience which is the hallmark of most funeral homes and cemeteries.

We shall give several examples of question "bombarding" stimulated by inner feelings of authority without further comment as the questions speak for themselves. Here goes: "Do you know the answer?" "Do you need more time to think?" "Do you realize there is a newspaper deadline?" "Can't you remember?" "Isn't there anyone you can call to get this?" "Do you know how important this insurance information is?" "You forgot the discharge papers – again?" "Didn't I make myself clear enough?" "Do you have the deed?" "Can you get the deed?" "When can you get the deed?" "Oh, did you remember the discharge papers?"

These are unbelievably all true questions that have been asked by funeral professionals over the years. Here is a good rule to go by: if you think you are bombarding the client family with questions, you are bombarding the client family with questions; slow down, regroup, heighten your own sensitivities and let go of the addiction to authority.

Authority in funeral/cemetery work has a 19th century concept that has long ago worn out its welcome!

How to Put the Desire for Authority in its Place: Put the Shoe on the Other Foot

Let me ask a question: how did any of us feel when people we turned to for gentle, kind help pulled out the authority card and played it to the hilt?

As odd as this is going to sound, I feel certain that we ought not to reply to every question or situation as being the ultimate funeral authority. In fact, I don't personally believe that the ultimate funeral authority even exists or ever existed for that matter.

It seems abundantly clear that our culture is crying out not for authority, but for relationships. There seems to be so many lonely people in the world, and hence, the consequences are even more magnified that funeral/cemetery professionals should seriously attempt a successful transformation for self-perceptions of being authority figures, as was certainly true some years ago, but instead create the reality of the transformation to servant, with a servant humble attitude towards the worthy ideal of being of service to others in a great time of need.

16. FORMS

"Oh my forms!" "I am up to here with forms!" "Oh the good ole' days when we make a sale on a handshake!" "This is all the monkey business of the lawyers!" Forms, forms, and then more forms!

Can we make an inventory of forms that are required or at least used in our profession? GPL, Casket Price List, Outer Enclosure Price List, Statement of Goods and Services, Embalming Case Report, Internment Order, Internment

Authorization, Hold Harmless agreements, Disclaimers, Clergy Record, Death Certificate, First-Call form, Social Security forms, Veterans Administration forms, IRS forms, ADA forms, Wage and Hour form, Release of Personal Property forms, Burial/Transit Permit, Christian Burial Permit, Floral and Remembrance forms, Music Selection forms, DOT forms, Payroll forms, Worker's Compensation forms, Annual Federal Tax Return forms, Asset Acquisition forms, Sales Tax report forms, OSHA forms, State Board forms. Well, you can probably add hundreds more to this list, but you get the general drift. We exist in a culture that has had an explosion of forms. Forms are everywhere.

I had open heart surgery a couple of months ago, and on one visit to the hospital to get ready to go under the knife, I was asked to fill out a four page form not just once, but was asked to complete the exact form - all four pages - four times in the same building. When I asked the hospital person why I was filling out the same four page form, four time she just shrugged her shoulders and mumbled something about "she didn't know why." Now to be fair the surgery was a success, the surgeon a genius and the nurses were heaven sent. I still however, don't know why I filled out the same form, four times in one day?

Now with all these tongue and cheek observations being made about the level of forms that infiltrate our lives, it is impossible to claim that our line of work, both funeral and cemetery service, does not include a true business contractual aspect to it that requires accuracy, legality and the written word, and oh yea, signatures, maybe a bunch of signatures.

It might even be possible to say that the funeral/cemetery financial experience is, in the end, a pure clear business transaction. Terms, conditions, prices, signatures, Social Security numbers, payment options are all a part of the final contract – so that seems to me to be a true and unblemished business agreement.

Because of this business reality inherent in the offering of goods and services to the public, there is the inevitable matter of forms (I must confess that for years I hated forms, and felt that it was a burden to my bereaved clients – Lord, was I wrong!)

Business forms, possibly forms of any type and kind, have historically in our beloved vocation been a cursed bane on the psychological health of scores of funeral and yes, cemetery professionals. Historically speaking, I believe it is safe to say that funeral professionals do not like forms. I believe it is safe to say that in the present day funeral professionals do not like forms any more than our ancestors did – they to be sure used them, but they didn't have a love affair with them.

The reasons for the dislike of forms are numerous, among them are: there seems no good time to fill them out, they take too long, mistakes have to be corrected, clients get impatient, you and I get impatient, it is embarrassing to calculate the cost of the goods and services in front of the client family (I mean doesn't it violate the sacredness of our great profession?), and even worse, all the time the "poor" bereaved family clients' are twiddling their thumbs in the conference room waiting, and waiting, and waiting while we are fiddling with these blasted forms. The result is that many of us do not like forms, but yet we have to fill them out, or else we will be in trouble with the state, the federal government, or worse, we might not get paid.

Because of this tension my thought is that we simply bite the bullet so to speak and have the necessary forms filled out during and as integral part of the service and sales process. At times this can be done quickly and unobtrusively. For example, "Before we move on Mr. Jones, there is a short form we must fill in. Should you have any reservations about any of the questions, please let me know as we come to them, and we'll try to see what's involved." In other words, instead of waiting as we were taught to tackle the forms at the very end of the conference, don't tackle them; take care of them throughout the interview conference, making the pesky forms an ally and not an enemy.

***CASE STUDY:** As odd as this story is going to sound, this was the way of things concerning the protocol and etiquette of handling the delicate duties of presenting a bereaved family their funeral bill way back in 1968. The firm I worked at was naturally on "unit" pricing (which meant the one number, usually in silver metal numbers – on the casket – covered everything.) When a client family would purchase a casket they got embalming, transfers, visitations, vehicles, everything – except of course, the cemetery charges, the certified copies of the death certificate, flowers, and other cash advance items. The problem was that the gentle tender protocol of the firm was that we would wait until three or four days after the funeral was over and formally make an appointment to see the family to formally present to them the final funeral bill. Of course, the fee in silver metal figures on the casket was by now added to many times by 100's of dollars for an ancillary purchases, and naturally and understandably most families did not keep a running tally as to just how much they had spent – we didn't even keep a running tally. The family found out how much they had actually spent when the funeral bill was presented to them in a blue velvet envelope – days after the burial had taken place (cremation was basically unheard of). Suffice to say, the concept of sticker shock was not exclusive to the automobile industry – I can well remember people's expressions being one of shock and dismay when they saw what they really owed.*

As controversial as the Funeral Rule of the Federal Trade Commission was when it was introduced, it did eliminate such overdone dramatics concerning the undertaker's delicate duties. To be fair, we truly, sincerely and honestly thought that our procedures in handling this financial obligation in such a manner was the absolute best for the grieving family. Never did I see any intentional fiddling with the funeral costs by the funeral professional, never. But of course, people like Jessica Mitford had other ideas about our professions integrity.

I have found most people, not all to be sure, but most people are patient people. Like my experience in filling out the same form, four times in one day. I find that people are conditioned, simply and possibly blindly, to submit to answering questions as an inevitability of life.

Unless, of course, they have been asked the same questions over and over again by different agencies or by different people in the same agency. Then, if they then balk, one can hardly blame them. In the end I did balk at the hospital and a firm letter was written. I felt very good after composing the letter, but of course, I never received a reply.

This situation should not be the case in any of us. If the client family can perceive from our behavior that he/she can state their reservations – that they can, so to speak, question our questions concerning absolutely anything concerning our services to them -then there should be little difficulty, provided that we as well can accept annoying funeral, cemetery and cremation forms as very important, and one of those pesky inevitabilities of living in the beginning of the 21st Century.

17. ENDINGS

Every funeral professional and cemeterian on the globe has heard this from clients: "Why?" "Why do we have to?"

Things have certainly changed since the days when the funeral director actually "directed" and people absolutely did what they were told. Of course this still happens, but as most everyone in our profession will readily attest, the publics comfort level with being told what to do by most anyone has changed considerably.

You know the routine: "Well, why do we need a vault?" "Why does the airlines require that?" "Why can't we bury Dad in his back yard?" "Why do you have all these forms?" "Why do we have to go in that room?" "Why don't you have coffee?" Why, why, why, why? We have always had the people addicted to the word "why" but I would suggest they are reproducing.

The single word that best symbolizes inquiry, suspicions, cynicisms, mistrust more than any other, and is most frequently employed in asking hard straight questions, is that little tiny word "why."

I want to confess that I have an aversion to the way the word is generally used, if not to the word itself, and it appears that this little word is being bantered around in the funeral service/cemetery profession more today than at any other time in our long and eventful history. For example, the case could easily be made and much could be said in support of the idea that the little word "why" is the genesis and motivation for all telephone shopping calls that we today routinely receive.

A legitimate basis for the use of the "why" word in our language undoubtedly exists, but I maintain that "why" has so often been misused in general communications that its original meaning has become distorted. It was once a word employed in the innocent search for information (which probably most telephone "shoppers" indeed are: innocent).

The word "why" signified the investigation of cause or reason. When employed in this manner even today, it is appropriate, and I know of no other word to take its place. Unfortunately, this is generally not the way it is used at our present time in funeral and cemetery service.

Today the word "why" too many times connotes disapproval and displeasure. Thus, when used by the funeral/cemetery professional or vice versa the client family, it communicates that something or somebody has done "wrong" or has behaved "badly." Even when that is not the meaning intended by the funeral/cemetery professional, that is generally how the word will be understood by us and vice versa.

The effect upon the client family will be predictably negative, for they will most probably have grown up in an environment in which "why" implied blame and condemnation. Naturally enough, they will react to the word in the funeral/cemetery experience the way they have learned to react to it over the years even though they may have used it simply in the sense of genuine inquiry. Thus, whenever the client family hears the word "why," they may feel the need to defend themselves, to withdraw and avoid the situation, or to attack.

In their early years, children use the word frequently – often to adult's utter frustration and distraction. "Why? Why? Why? Why?" For them it is a key to unlock the secrets of the world about them; it enables them to explore and discover. They ask for information without implying moral judgment, approval or disapproval. They learn from asking why.

In time, however they learn that the adults surrounding them use the word differently. The child learns that adults use the "why" word to put them on the spot, to show them they are behaving in an unacceptable manner. Slowly but surely the children stop using the word for the purpose of inquiry and begin to employ it against others the very same way it has been used against them.

The child's ears ring with the questions from accusatory adults: "Why did you muddy my clean floor?" "Why are you barefoot?" "Why don't you use your knife and fork properly?" "Why did you break that dish?" etc., etc. Children learn to imitate their elders. Soon enough they will say to their friend, "Why did you take my bike?" "Why did you play with my 'stuff?'" to show that they disapprove of the act and not because they are interested in obtaining a bit of useful information. The child will say to the mother, "Why must I go to the store?" not because they want a reason but because they don't wish to go. This is the child's way of saying, "No, I am against it."

The funeral/cemetery professional should, as best as possible, avoid and be wary of using the word "why." But what about when the client family uses it?

As mentioned before our profession has heard the word "why" more in the last quarter of a century that in the previous five hundred years. Client families use "why" a great deal. "Why do we need that?" "Why should we buy that?" "Why is this so much money?" "Why can't we just . . . . ?" "Why can't I bury Mom on top of Mount Rushmore, I mean this is America?" The word why is today a permanent part of the process of the funeral/cemetery interview for us all basically in most interactions in sales and service.

Should the word "why," then, never be used? I know I wish I would employ it less, for in spite of all my reservations and objections to its use, it keeps cropping up. I try to avoid it and am glad when I succeed, but often enough there it is to be dealt with again. That one little word, however, does have a justifiable place, and this is the one additional point I want to make. If the client family perceives that our attitude is unthreatening, if we have established trust and respect, and then if we use "why" simply to obtain factual information that the client family possesses, then our use of the word should not cause undue damage. Perhaps I am saying this to comfort and solace ourselves as most everyone continues asking "why," but I hope this point is indeed legitimate.

For all the reasons given above, I feel that we should use "why" as sparingly as possible and that when we do use it, we should do so to get at facts rather than feelings, and thoughts rather than emotions. For example, no one in our profession, outside an insane asylum, would ever ask, "Well, why do you feel that way?" That question my friends is an absolute guarantee for unwanted and unnecessary trouble.

In our culture facts and thoughts are more readily accessible, more easily disclosed, than feelings and emotions. As funeral/cemetery professionals it is our responsibility to furnish answers, and good solid, answers to all the "whys" that come our way

NAVIGATION QUESTIONS THAT FUNERAL PROFESSIONALS ASK
- ### IS COUNSELING MORE THAN GIVING SYMPATHY?

A funeral counselor would naturally be sympathetic to what is happening to the person which whom we are serving and working with. However, it is my conviction that our interest in the bereaved should be much deeper than sympathy. The dictionary tells us that sympathy is a "sameness of feeling" or the "ability to enter into another's mental or emotional state, especially pity or compassion for another's trouble or suffering". A funeral professional cannot expect to have the sameness of feeling with those we serve, although we may well and sincerely feel compassion that moves us to really try to help them.

This is an important thing to keep in mind when working with the bereaved. We do not have to have their feelings in order to recognize their right to have the feelings they have.

A physician does not have to have every symptom of the patient to understand how much the patient is suffering. A nurse does not have to have the patient's pain in order to do their work, and certainly a dentist does not have to have a toothache to know just how much it hurts. A lawyer does not have to break all the laws in order to help a client with a law suit, not does a pastor have to commit every sin in order to know the value of confession.

Likewise the funeral professional does not have to be in grief to understand and help the grieving person. Funeral professionals almost universally have a deeper concerning for what is happening in the grieved person, and we want to do something to relieve their distress. A funeral professional is naturally sympathetic, but hopefully we are also much more.

- **CAN A FUNERAL PROFESSIONAL REALLY DO ANY COUNSELING IN A FORMAL ARRANGEMENT CONFERENCE?**

I once sat down with a group of veteran funeral professionals who had been engaged in the professional for at least twenty years each to discuss the funeral arrangement conference. We talked about it and their experience with it for four solid days. When that session was over I reaffirmed as to just how much actual counseling happens even though some of the participants disliked the word "counseling."

There are three reasons why I believe this:

First, in a time of special need people tend to be open to suggestions and guidance – which is a central core of the funeral arrangement conference. The funeral professional, most times, is selected by free-choice because there is a belief that they can be trusted to serve the well-being of people. Funeral professional's virtue of being available serves as an instrumental force serving as a special guide in managing the crisis that brought the bereaved together in the first place. It was clear that these veteran funeral professionals were counseling all the time and had been doing it for years, even though they did not call it counseling.

Second, the funeral arrangement conference is by its very nature designed to make a variety of decisions that are important for the bereaved. Decision making situations are the times when guidance and wise counsel are most appropriately given and received, and funeral professionals do this task constantly.

Third, the funeral arrangement conference usually involves several persons and so, the basic elements for group counseling exist. Psychological movement tends to be more rapid in a group, for usually ideas stimulate communication, and being together at an important time of decision making gives the funeral professional an added opportunity for the counseling process.

Interestingly, this learned group of funeral professionals did offer one innovative suggestion. They all concluded that the phrase "funeral arrangement conference" sounded too business like, too formal, and too distant. They came up with a new phrase for this important event: <u>THE HELPING INTERVIEW.</u>

- **DOES A FUNERAL PROFESSIONAL HAVE A RIGHT TO BE A COUNSELOR?**

As a member of a recognized care-providing profession, funeral professionals have not only the right, but the obligation to be counselors. Funeral professionals most often touch the lives of people when they are in great need. The funeral professional's sensitivity to these needs may in the end have a significant bearing on the happiness and the health of the bereaved for years to come. This should be totally understood, and not ever underestimated! The helping relationship between the funeral professional and the bereaved in the community exists as a fact of life. The funeral professional functioning within that relationship certainly requires understanding and skill in human relations and in the end, this is basic to wise counseling.

- **"I DON'T BELIEVE IN COUNSELING. I DON'T THINK THIS IT IS A FUNERAL DIRECTORS JOB. WHAT DO YOU SAY TO A PERSON LIKE ME? I MEAN, I DON'T WANT TO GET SUED!"**

I say this is an easy dodge, and it doesn't work. As mentioned before, several times, we don't have a choice as a funeral professional as to whether or not we even believe in counseling, let alone embrace it. Whenever you work with people in a time of crisis you automatically become a counselor. The only choice you have is whether or not you will be a wise and helpful counselor or not.

When funeral professionals say they don't believe in counseling what they are really doing is saying that there is a part of the role of a funeral professional that they want to avoid.

This question begs comment as it is encountered in the funeral field, but most effective and sensitive funeral professionals already know that counseling, and wise, valid, and careful counseling is simply a major part of taking on the role of a funeral professional.

- **SHOULD A FUNERAL PROFESSIONAL REFER TO THEMSELVES AS A GRIEF COUNSELOR OR A GRIEF THERAPIST?**

Usually it is wise to avoid fancy titles. If a funeral professional is confident and secure in what they are doing that is the important thing. Interestingly, often people resist counseling if they think or know that is what is going on, but welcome it if they feel it is a friendly conversation with a concerned friend. The process of funeral counseling and the funeral rituals is the important thing, not the name that is given to it.

- **THESE DAYS, PEOPLE WANT THE FUNERAL OVER AND DONE AS QUICKLY AS POSSIBLE. HOW CAN ANY COUNSELING TAKE PLACE WHEN YOU ARE WITH A FAMILY SUCH A SHORT TIME, SOMETIMES JUST A COUPLE OF HOURS?**

As frustrating as the abbreviated funeral experience can be, it is well to remember that people will care for their dead in a consistent manner with how they live their lives, and people live fast lives. It should also be helpful to remember that not all time is the same. At least, emotional time is relative. In times of crisis there may be very rapid emotional activity. To be there at this critical time is important but it is also advantageous. The funeral professional, no matter the length of time, is usually with the bereaved during prime time as far as counseling opportunity is concerned. So, it is not necessarily a matter of how much time you have with the bereaved as it is to how well prepared you are to use this prime time to be best advantage of the bereaved served.

Also, there are ways of extending time. Dr. Erich Lindemann, the late professor of psychiatry at Harvard Medical School, pointed out when I was a student that the most difficult time for many bereaved people comes ten days to two weeks after the death. Relatives have gone home and friends have many times returned to their interests. And the thousand and one little things that remind one of the loss are so often times faced alone.

The concerned insightful funeral counselor will and can find a reason for stopping by at the home. Often times this one visit opens up a much needed chance for the bereaved to talk out feelings with the funeral professional who has been already close during the time of crisis. Usually this type of interest is appreciated and interpreted as genuine concern.

This simple idea of extending time is the heart and soul of aftercare programs.

- **WHAT DO CEREMONIES DO FOR PEOPLE?**

This is an excellent question for a funeral professional to ask!

Healthy ceremonies are worthy of such a classification when they serve a useful, healthful purpose for a majority of the people in any given community.

Ceremonies provide an appropriate setting in which people can easily express legitimate feelings relating to important events in their lives, or in the life of the group. For instance, a funeral in the Italian community in Boston's North End, will be very different from a funeral in the Methodist community located in Iowa.

A funeral will serve as a healthy ceremony when it helps the individuals in a community accept rather than deny their far-reaching feelings; moreover, it serves healthful ends when it is conducted in an atmosphere that permits facing reality, not only personally, but socially. When a number of other people accept a fact it is increasingly difficult for one or two members of the group to deny it.

A funeral can actually make it possible for the group to verify its faith in the future by saying, in effect, "We also know what is happening to you, for most of us have been through it ourselves." Unfortunately, private funeral ceremonies so limit the community's involvement that this faith in the future is usually greatly diluted or missed entirely.

I once served a gentleman whose wife had died. He was adamant that he wanted nothing concerning ceremony and ritual. I gently tried to persuade him that he might simply want to place an obituary in the paper to let the community know what had happened, and he immediately in anger accused me of getting "kickbacks" from the newspaper. So nothing was done to confront and announce to the world what had happened to him. In a month he was back in my office ready to pay the expenses incurred in disposing of his wives remains. He looked at me with an expression of such pain and despair and said this: "You really know who your friends are when something bad happens to you. You know, not one person, not one person has called, written or stopped by to see me." I once again suggested that it was not too late to put something in the newspaper and I again, for my own protection, assured him that I was not on the newspapers underground payroll. The poor man agreed to the obituary. Months later I ran into him in downtown Omaha and he greeted me with a big smile. When the obituary was finally published, the community (who had concluded by the absence of an obituary that this man wanted to be alone) interpreted the news as an invitation to express their concern. And express it they did. Cards and letter flooded in, cakes, pies, cookies, casseroles, and telephone calls arrived daily. The community liked this man and they were genuinely concerned about him, and once the door was opened by implementing the ceremonial event we call an obituary, the community gladly crossed the threshold of sympathetic understanding and sent this man, by thought and by action, a mighty powerful message – YOU ARE NOT ALONE! As a footnote about the English word OBITUARY, it comes to us from two sources. In Latin, the word OBITUS means death and in Greek, the word OBITUPOLOS means "a cry for help."

The ceremony depends on its efficacy not so much on what it says as it does on the group's expression of its own experiences, and on the recognized, ritualized expressions of faith and feelings. When words fail, people use rituals across the globe. In this way there is verification of one's ability to find the way through such devastating an experience as the death of a loved one. Private funerals rarely accomplish these important tasks in the search for healing.

This ability to communicate thought and feeling through acts that are commonly understood gives to the funeral its special value.

- **WHY DO PEOPLE GET SO EMOTIONALLY UPSET WHEN THE SUBJECT OF DEATH IS RAISED?**

This question assumes a universal response that I do not believe to be invariably true. Mature men and women, who have thought about death, and who have developed a well thought out philosophy of both life and death, can think and talk about death quite casually and without personal apprehension. But it takes time, thought, and effort to develop this life asset.

The groups which have mature attitudes towards death, however, is minimal in our population. It is quite true that for many, in fact the majority of contemporary human beings, the whole subject of death are fraught with anxiety and discomfort such as the subject of sex was viewed 100 years ago. This may be caused by a number of things. Sometimes it is caused by childhood experiences when death was not talked about nor confronted and so, became especially distressing to contemplate as an adult. For others the mention of death may immediately recall one particular death that was so poorly managed that it created emotional damage which has never been accepted and hence, not dealt with. For example, a car driven by a friend of mine struck and killed a woman who stepped out from between two parked cars. My friend was unable to avoid the accident, and this fact was clearly established without question by the police and by a court that investigated the accident. He was never charged with anything legally. However, his emotions were charged so greatly that even now, many years later, the mention of death, any death, still triggers memories for my friend of that horrible moment when he saw what was happening in his life and was helpless to do anything about it.

The mention of death also is a stark reminder about our own fate, and this is in itself quite distressing for people who have not developed an understanding of the meaning of their own existence. To think about death when one is not sure of the meaning of their life is bound to be upsetting.

- **WHAT DOES A FUNERAL HAVE TO DO WITH THE DIGNITY OF HUMANITY?**

The way various cultures treat the bodies of those who have died tends to reflect their philosophy as to the innate worth and dignity of the entire human family and experience. In a society where, for example, the state decides who is important and who is not, the irreverent and reckless care of the dead is common place. Nazi Germany's treatment of the Jewish dead during the Second World War is a premier example of this fact. In fact, throughout history civilization have in part been gauged and evaluated as to their advancement concerning the dignity of human beings by how they care for their dead.

There is an alarming pattern in contemporary American culture to disregard the dead. We hide them from sight, to dispose of them and quickly as possible, and to spend the least amount of time in their presence. This pattern of disregard threatens the whole idea of the human's special quality to attest that life is more than just a biological event. When the body that has served as the physical residence of the spirit is treated with disregard, disrespect, and disinterest on the part of the living, the basic assumptions that we cherish about life named regard, respect and interest are challenged.

The care we show for the dead is really then, a means we employ to guarantee respect for life. Reverence for life has on the flip side reverence for the dead. Indeed, what we are talking about here is a matter of the value we place upon life itself. If we make any part of the human experience – birth, childhood, adulthood, old age – any part of it cheap we cheapen all the rest of it. It is regrettably easier to downgrade respect for human nature than to build it up again.

For a long period of time we quite naturally and tenaciously clung to values that dignified the human innate qualities of being. Today, however, we are certainly gazing with dismay on contemporary practices that allow for this basic respect, regard and interest to wither away.

If death is anything, it is democratic. The Grim Reaper is the best example of an equal opportunity employer in existence. When we look at how we care for the dead, we are also looking into a moral mirror of how we take care of the living. Sometimes the reflection in the mirror is hopeful and optimistic, sometimes, many times, today, it is not.

- **YOU TALK A LOT ABOUT CEREMONIES. WHY ARE CEREMONIES SO IMPORTANT?**

Ceremonies are usually elaborate ways of doing things that really don't have to be done at all except to satisfy important emotional needs.

I am of the professional conviction that the rites, rituals and ceremonies, what human beings have called for centuries "the funeral", is the absolute minimal core of what makes up the value, purpose, and benefit of the experience of the funeral in the first place.

The absence of rites, rituals and ceremonies when a death occurs has significant consequences. The consequences of such an attitude to funeral service and humanity as a whole is devastating. As the great psychologist Eric Erickson said "No community can survive without rituals."

Removing rites, rituals and ceremonies, the funeral professional's very purpose and career description, is severely diluted to the point that the funeral professional becomes a simple disposer of the dead.

Rites, rituals and ceremonies are critical, and here is why.

It is certainly easy and possible to get a diploma without attending elaborate commencement exercise, but nonetheless "graduation days" are wonderful occasions, particularly for the parents who paid the bill, which mark important milestones in life.

A couple can be just as legally married by obtaining a license and having a justice of the peace mutter a few legal words, yet many thousands of people are not satisfied with just that. They choose instead to spend hundreds, or even many thousands of dollars that might otherwise be invested or used for furnishing the home, to have a big wedding with many friends in attendance, a grand reception with an expensive dinner and flowers, gowns, and much, much more. They take pictures of it so that they will never forget this wonderful moment. None of this wedding ceremony is legally necessary, but it serves an important purpose in the lives of the participants. They seek to surround a most important event in their life with all the meaning, dignity, tradition and joy they can employ. What is absolutely amazing is they do all of this and the divorce rate is 53%. Spend $20,000 or $200,000 and the marriage lasts a year. However, people still do the ceremony.

Actually, as with most ceremonies, it is an investment in meaning, not permanency. It is perhaps difficult to justify in terms of hard dollars and cents, yet so important to the emotional needs of the participants that wherever you find human beings you will find elaborate ceremonies, made lavish with an extravagance that reason alone won't easily justify.

I remember all the times I have watched the changing of the guards and Buckingham Palace, or the ceremonies at the Royal Horse Guards, or watching Princess Diana's funeral on television, or even reruns of the coronation of Queen Elizabeth with all the great pomp and ceremony and simply being enthralled with the sophistication of the British rituals. Of course, I know very well that the English monarch has not really had any political power for centuries, but that logic and rational view means nothing to me when I am caught up in the splendor of the ceremony.

It may be the simple baptism of a little baby in a small village church with its quiet joy; the meaning of the social ceremony has its value ultimately not in what it costs (however, no one should ever go into debt over a ceremony) but in what it does for the participants.

Rites, rituals and ceremonies define our level of civilization.

PART II

The Principles of Funeral Service Counseling

The basic needs of the grief stricken need to be met in such a way that people can move through their crises and not get bogged down in them. As funeral directors who serve the bereaved, we want to help families emerge as whole and restored persons rather than as diminished and damaged individuals. From this perspective, the work of the funeral professional aligns itself much more on the professional/ministerial side than it does on the merchant/business side.

This book is not designed to include counseling techniques, philosophies, theories, or attending skills. The mission of this book is to identify and explain the various principles which make up funeral service counseling.

THE FOUNDATION OF FUNERAL COUNSELING

Funeral service counseling is a process that helps people work through their problems when death enters their lives. Death creates many different kinds of problems and nearly all of them have potentially serious emotional dimensions. In exploring the principles of funeral counseling, we need to give attention to several foundations which sets our path in the question of improving our own skills in fulfilling this important role.

THE HELPING PROFESSIONS – IS FUNERAL SERVICE ONE OF THEM?

Dr. Albert Schweitzer, the world famous medical missionary said this concerning service to humanity, "I don't know what your destiny will be, but one thing I know; the only ones among you who will be really happy are those who have sought and found how to serve."

I have long held that this definition fits our beloved profession like a glove. In fact, the very name of our profession "funeral service" includes service in its title. Service to others always seems to be magnified by the extent of the problems that other people are facing. If this evaluation is accurate then funeral service as a profession is a mission driven career in which helping people solve their problems when death enters their lives becomes the core, the epicenter, the nucleus of our lives as funeral professionals.

Let's explore this idea of helping people with problems a little further.

For instance, a lawyer helps people resolve the legal problems that distress them. A physician helps relieve the physical problems that cause suffering. The clergy work with the spiritual problems that bother people. The teacher works with educational problems.

The funeral professional helps people resolve the problems that surround the events of death. Given that the death rate is 100%, the type of help that funeral professionals offer is extremely important.

There has been somewhat of a debate over the years about whether or not funeral professionals are true authentic counselors. Dr. Rollo May in his classic book "The Art of Counseling" points out that anyone who helps a person through a life crisis is really a counselor. As he puts it, "personal counseling is any deep understanding between persons that results in a changing of personality." (p. 120). The relief of suffering produces a change in personality. Clearly then, the work of the funeral professionals, whose very mission in life is to help relieve some of the misery that death creates, falls within the boundaries of Dr. May's definition.

In the funeral counseling and the entire funeral process, people reflect their fears, curiosity, and concerns. These in return are invitations for information, insight, and understanding which the funeral professional is specially trained to offer.

Often the first questions from a family are tentative and exploratory. They indicate a deeper feeling that needs to be understood and explored. People come to a funeral professional voluntarily with the questions that trouble them about death, grief, and the funeral. Funeral professionals are also usually the first professional people that the bereaved talk to after a death. This is a wise method of coping with problems for the funeral professional can and does ease their doubts, fears, and uncertainties.

This then, is a description of the process of funeral counseling. It involves the quest for information, guidance, suggestions, understanding, insight, reassurance, and options. It opens the doors for healthful action, relief of stress and emotional growth.

Counseling in funeral service is important because it helps people cope with the death crisis that disrupts life if unwisely managed. We usually think that a crises happen outside of us - the accident, the fatality, the murder or the suicide may seem outside of us. But the emotional crisis of loss is always deep inside of the person who has attachments to the external event.

These emotional crises can cause a special type of pain. Grief emotions can and do shake a person's security system and his or her control mechanisms may be shattered. The person so affected will show the physical and emotional symptoms of their distress. They will ache, feel mental distress, emotional disturbance and basically be filled with self-doubts. One's whole life may be turbulent and uncertain as if he or she were caught off balance and could not right the situation again.

As hard and as difficult as this idea is, it is none the less absolutely true; the resources for ultimately restoring one's balance must come from within. No one can see for anyone else, breathe for another, or even suffer for another. But in a grief crisis, and more specifically a death crisis, there can be a temporary process where help is given. An example would be that Cardio Pulmonary Resuscitation (CPR) helps a person carry on the function of breathing temporarily with outside help. When vision is obscured by circumstance, others can guide us. And talking about a loss can ease suffering, and this is precisely the goal of funeral service counseling.

Dr. Rollo May says, "The counselor should not relieve his or her counselee of suffering, but rather redirect his or her suffering into constructive channels." (p. 159). Instead of denying that the suffering exists, the funeral profession in funeral counseling tries to find with the bereaved a meaning in the loss that can sustain life. Many people are broken by death and loss, while others are made wiser and better through it. By being a primary guide in the death crisis, funeral professionals keep their eye on the goal of bringing forth and developing inner resources that can enrich life and give meaning even to life's most distressing event.

Funeral counseling is important because it does not seek a superficial approach to the deep problems of life. Funeral service, through rites, rituals, and ceremonies, seeks out wisdom and understanding to help provide the strong resources that are essential for meeting the crises that death creates. As funeral professionals, you have often heard people say, "I did not know how I was going to get through those days, but the funeral helped me so much I found new strength deep inside." Such words imply that a wise and helpful funeral professional was at work. This is a major goal in the funeral profession and is the purpose of this book.

POSSIBLY THE MOST DIFFICULT QUESTION A HUMAN BEING CAN ASK – "WHO AM I?"

Who are we, as funeral directors, to be identified as persons to help the grieving? How do we help the grieving, and what are the easiest and most economically sensible resources that we have at our disposal, right now, to help bereaved families meet their emotional needs?

In the beginning of trying to answer the question of "who am I?" I would like to draw the reader's attention to two facts concerning funeral professionals that I believe are absolutely true: first, they possess a tremendous amount of experiential expertise, which is equal and in many cases surpasses even the most rigorous academic accomplishments, and second, that funeral counseling does not exclusively depend on high level academic achievements, instead funeral counseling mostly depends on the simple and very ethereal idea of someone helping someone else with a problem. It is this simple approach to counseling that this book will follow.

So, who am I as a funeral professional to be counseling anyway? You may well ask a very valid question such as "I mean, isn't counseling just for doctors, and therapists?" or "I always thought you had to go to college for years to be able to counsel someone." The answer to these questions is simple: NO. You don't have to have endless academic degrees to do counseling, and certainly counseling is not just the exclusive territory of doctors and therapists. As was stated in the previous paragraph, this book centers on a simple definition of counseling which is anytime anybody helps anybody with a problem.

This is not to discount education and training, and this book will absolutely encourage any funeral professional to pursue further educational experiences and attainments. All advanced education and training for any funeral professional which translates into enhanced care of bereaved families is a good thing.

However, when I was in seminary, we did not have one course in the psychology of grief, bereavement counseling or sociology of death and dying, and the seminary I attended was not the exception - it was the rule! Hence, even the ordained clergy who minister to be bereaved mostly operate under our definition of counseling – anytime anybody helps anybody else with a problem.

The truth is that all Mortuary College curriculums require almost 25% of the course work to be precisely in the areas of psychology of grief, bereavement counseling and sociology of death and dying. The case could easily be made that by adding the typical funeral professionals experiential expertise to the academic requirements required to graduate from a mortuary college, the typical contemporary funeral professional emerges as the most learned professional in the community when it comes to taking on the responsibility of being a counselor to the bereaved.

In fact, as funeral professionals we really don't have the option of asking the question "am I a counselor?" The only question funeral professionals can really ask is "will I be a wise and insightful counselor?" It has been my observation in my career that many times in life, simple things are made extraordinarily complicated, and I would suggest that this has sometimes happened in defining the funeral professional's duties and responsibilities in the realm of counseling.

I have tried to simplify this complication by identifying five qualities that every human being in funeral service already possess, even though they might not be aware of these assets, or even if they are licensed or not – everybody in the funeral profession has these qualities at their fingertips.

Here they are:
1. Funeral counselors are people to talk to.
2. Funeral counselors give people something to do.
3. Funeral counselors give people ways to express feelings.
4. Funeral counselors give people something to hold on to.
5. Funeral counselors give people something to believe in.

Let's explore these five important funeral counselor qualities one by one:

1. FUNERAL COUNSELORS ARE PEOPLE TO TALK TO

Whenever we are faced with a tragic circumstance, there is a strong impulse to put the experience into words, to talk it out. This is vital to the process of facing reality of the situation, such as the death of a loved one. Hearing our own words, telling our own story, has a way of convincing our inner realm of feelings as to what has truly happened to us. The wise helping process of the funeral ritual is basically built upon the process of talking. This is the reason that times of funeral arrangements, wakes, public calling hours, Shiva, are so valuable. During these planned times people simply talk. Probably nothing earth shattering or profound will be said, the conversations will not change the political landscape of the country, but emotional healing will take place – it is basically how the therapy of the funeral ritual works. People in crisis usually seek someone who can understand their turbulent feelings and their efforts to put their feelings into words. This is the basic reason why phone lines are jammed in the aftermath of a crisis and/or disaster. Often, this process of understanding is essentially a form of people together discussing situations and the funeral professional using perceptive listening. A skillful listener, who is not threatened or fearful by what he or she hears becomes a sounding board against which the bereaved bounces his or her ideas, until they begin to make sense. The funeral arrangement conference and conversation provides an unusual opportunity to provide this form of relationship building, communication and beginning healing.

Most people confronted with the problems that are created by death discover that talking the problems out is a highly effective way to deal wisely with them. In times of the death crisis, people are urged to ease their burden by sharing them with others who are specially trained to help them cope. **_THIS IS REALLY WHAT FUNERAL SERVICE COUNSELING IS ALL ABOUT._**

CASE STUDY: *The issue of talking out problems and stresses is easily observable in any funeral home. I have labelled this process the "Tape Recorder Syndrome" and it works this way.*

The funeral professional sometimes greets the bereaved with this question "I'm so sorry for your loss, how did it happen?" Then the bereaved tell their story "I woke up at 2:30 a.m. and heard Fred coughing, by the time I called 911 he was unconscious, and he died on the trip to the hospital."

The next person, say at the visitation, greets the same bereaved and inquires "How did it happen?" and once again the bereaved will start out with "I woke up at 2:30 a.m. and heard Fred coughing ...," and repeats verbatim the same exact story.

These repetitions of the same story can easily be told hundreds of times, using the same words, in the exact same sequence.

This pattern of repetition is extremely valuable for by repeated self-talk and doing it in a group supportive setting, the bereaved begins to actually believe what they themselves are saying.

This process usually takes place during the calling hours or time of sharing at the funeral home. This process does not take place as readily if the bereaved isolate themselves from group support.

One of the hallmark skills that most funeral counselors possess is a genuine, sincere and keen sense in the basic human skill of listening.

2. FUNERAL COUNSELORS GIVE PEOPLE SOMETHING TO DO

All societies and cultures surround life crises with acting-out ceremonies that we call rites and rituals. This is the basic idea behind all funeral activities. The funeral rituals is a premier example of a cultural universal. There is no place on earth where people don't do funerals.

These acting-out ceremonies are easily accessible to everyone, and may well be the most useful resources for acting out or expressing deep feelings that are too painful, difficult, or even impossible to put into words alone. A wise rabbi once told me, "When words fail, people turn to rituals."

The need to do things at the time of crises gently leads a person into a kind of relationship which forms a communication that a person might not easily engage in if the opportunity for a ritual was not provided. Every culture, whether contemporary or primitive, surrounds the crises of life with acting out ceremonies.

At birth, adolescence, marriage, as well as educational, political and historical events, and also at the time of death, people used rites, rituals, and ceremonies to attempt to embrace and cope with the rapid changes that these rites of passage create.

Rituals provide important things that people can do to help work through the feelings associated with the event. Ritual and ceremonies are important and helpful activities that people can participate in to help work through the feelings associated with these significant and sometimes critical events.

THESE ACTING-OUT, OR RITUAL PROCESSES HAVE THREE THINGS IN COMMON:

FIRST: THEY SHARE A COMMON FORM OF COMMUNICATION THAT EVERYONE UNDERSTANDS.

CASE STUDY: The following example of common forms of communication that is understood by everyone illustrates the uniqueness that every funeral ritual exhibits.

I was born and raised in the Midwest, where most grief and mourning practices were very restrained and subdued. Rarely did people fall apart at funerals - usually the people I was raised around put on the strongest persona they could. While this restrained grieving was common practice, it definitely had its limitations, for an inordinate number of widows and widowers in my community were often cranky, ill-tempered, and distant. However, for good or for ill, this was the form of communication that everyone understood to be "normal" and that's how it was.

When I was twenty years old, I moved to Boston to attend Mortuary College. I took room and board with an Italian Catholic funeral director on the North Shore, and the form of communication that everyone understood at Italian funerals in Boston was significantly different from what I understood to be "normal" in the Midwest.

First, in the Italian community at funerals and wakes, people laughed, argued, cried, and even fainted! The participants at these funerals in Boston were much more expressive, dramatic, emotional, and volatile that I had seen back home in the ultra-conservative Midwest.

The Italian community in Boston expressed its grief in a big way. They were not emotionally constrained or restrained. At wakes, a healthy and very impressive series of human events took place. Feelings were not repressed, they were without inhibition expressed.

Usually, the funeral home chapel was packed with flowers, literally wall to wall. Active behaviors included, arguing, making up, eating, drinking, sobbing some more, laughing, and staying at the funeral home for hours. The Italian culture in Boston expressed their feelings!

The common form of communication seen as "normal" between the Italian community in Boston and my Midwestern friends' was glaring. The Italians in Boston were not as cranky, ill-tempered or distant as were the people in the Midwest after the funeral was over.

SECOND: ACTING OUT PROCESSES USUALLY CENTERS ON A FORMAL OR INFORMAL PARADE WHICH HAS DEEP SIGNIFICANCE FOR ALL WHO ARE CONCERNED.

EXAMPLE: "EVERYBODY LOVES A PARADE"

For example, when a child loses a pet, if the adults, and this is a big if, allow the child to express his or her inner needs, the child will implement a parade in the burial ceremonies for the dead pet. Without ever having gone to a funeral, children will instinctually initiate a parade when a significant event happens in their lives.

It is the same in times of crisis with people who absolutely need to "parade or process." Nearly every significant event in life is signified and imprinted in our brains by having a parade. It may be the Macy's Thanksgiving Day Parade, a processional for a wedding, or a procession or parade to a cemetery. Regardless of the form, the ability to parade allows for a nonverbal expression of the significance of the event people are involved with.

The statement is often heard that "I don't want people **PARADING** around me when I'm dead." While this idea may sound attractive, it contains two significant limitations.

First, the very term "funeral" is derived from the word "**funeralis**" which in Latin means a "torch light procession or parade." The funeral is one of the oldest processions or parades known to history.

Second, there is an ancient and well-recognized value in the concept of a human beings making or being involved actively in making a final pilgrimage.

Throughout life, significant events are signaled by a pilgrimage or parade or human beings. This can be walking down a church aisle to be married, marching in a St. Patrick's Day Parade, Christ's pilgrimage to Calvary, or viewing a casket and decedent during a file by at a funeral ritual. Regardless of the type of procession or recession, the concept of the parade is significant and should not be underestimated.

THIRD, ACTING OUT EVENTS, RITUALS EMPLOY ALL LEVELS OF HUMAN RESPONSE, BODY, MIND, AND SOUL. ONE OF THE MOST SIGNIFICANT ASPECTS OF THE FUNERAL IS THE FACT THAT IT INVOLVES THE TOTAL HUMAN IN RESPONSE TO THE EVENT.

The funeral implements the human *body* in two ways:
1. The Dead Body is used as the ultimate visible symbol of the life which has lived, and
2. The Living Body (the live mourners) who actively participates in the ritual by walking, talking, lifting, carrying, moving, etc.

The funeral implements the human *mind* by:
1. The mental expression of deep grief feelings,
2. The mental realization about what has actually happened and exploring what it means, and
3. The development of mental solutions to reenter the mainstream of life.

The funeral implements the human *soul* by:
1. Helping interpret the event of death,
2. Expressing the various belief systems of the bereaved and involved individuals,
3. Expressing emotions that accompany these beliefs, and
4. Giving way to overt conduct expressing these beliefs and emotions through rites, rituals, and ceremonies.

The simple idea of doing something is of great importance. When people are not able to wisely act out their feelings, do something about the feelings, then the feelings often times take detours inwards and produce the organic and pathological acting-out that we call illness, or the detour creates types of personality modification that we call mental or emotional illness.

3. FUNERAL COUNSELORS GIVE PEOPLE WAYS TO EXPRESS FEELINGS

The need to express feelings needs to be supported by the setting within which the expression of feelings is valid and appropriate. For example, expressing deep feelings of grief at a funeral home, church, or private home is valid and appropriate -but expressing such feelings at a baseball game, at a public movie, or in the aisle of a grocery store in the midst of surprised strangers can be invalid and inappropriate. Important resources in meeting crises must stimulate the expression of valid feelings. Military service has been said to stimulate the works of heroic acts in historical and social events. Romantic people stimulate the tender emotions that may be expressed at a romantic encounter or a wedding. Funeral acting out rituals, special services, and funeral music and funeral colors are used at death occasions to stimulate the expression of the feelings that are appropriate in times of sorrow and tragedy. Even paid mourners have in times past been used to create the atmosphere for pouring out sad feelings. Not only the music, but also the decor, architecture and those other factors that help create "atmosphere" should be "responsive to" the situation.

The chance to express strong feelings without restraint or inhibition serves a therapeutic purpose. For the alternative is repression with the unhealthy and unfortunate effects that accompany the denial of emotion. The funeral home "atmosphere" quite adequately fulfills all these needs to express grief emotions in a valid and appropriate manner.

CASE STUDY: THE PRESSURE COOKER

I was called to respond to the death of a middle-aged man. When I arrived at the residence, the widow was the picture of composure and control. Her husband's death had not been unexpected she told me, however, she confessed she was a little surprised that he died as fast as he did.

At the funeral conference, her self-imposed self-control was still in fine form and she instructed me that there would be no calling hours, and she would plan the memorial service at a later date--on her own. She did not want the funeral home or the funeral professional involved.

The funeral home I was operating at the time also operated an emergency ambulance service.

It was about eight months later after the death of this gentleman that I received a call requesting our ambulance come to a small department store downtown. The person requesting the ambulance told us that a lady was "going nuts" in his store; the police were already on the scene.

When we arrived on the scene, it actually took me a while to recognize the hysterical woman as the same widow whose husband's death we had taken care of to eight months ago.

To say the very least, this woman now was in a bad way. She later told her physician that she felt like a pressure cooker was boiling inside ever since she knew of her husband's fatal diagnosis. She said at the beginning of her grief she truly thought she could hold it in and be the paragon of strength. As time passed, however, she began to feel an impending explosion and what she encountered at the department store ignited here emotional fuse.

In the department store she walked past the record section. As she was browsing through the records she saw an album by Dean Martin. Dean Martin was her husband's favorite singer.

As she stared at the Dean Martin record album she described a pressure cooker volcano-type feeling which was boiling inside her and she could not hold it in, and she just exploded. She burst into tears, smashed the Dean Martin album, and then started throwing all the rest of the records like Frisbees around the store.

The owners of the store and other customers were utterly terrified and mortified, and did not in the least comprehend what was going on, nor should they have been expected to do so.

Had this emotional pressure been released within the funeral home environment, had a funeral professional been in attendance, the outburst would have been appropriate, valid, expected and MOST IMPORTANT OF ALL - IT WOULD HAVE BEEN UNDERSTOOD.

As it was, this poor soul had basically delayed her healing a lengthy eight months by denying and working against the reality of death. If she had expressed her emotions openly, as difficult as that might well have been, at the time of her husband's death in a safe and appropriate place in the presence of people who truly understood, she would have had by the time of her explosion eight months to process and explore this loss experience and hence, be all that closer to possibly some type of beginning healing.

4. FUNERAL COUNSELORS GIVE PEOPLE SOME ONE TO HOLD ON TO

One of the more severe effects of the emotional crises concerning death is the sense of rapid, turbulent change, and the infusion of new people into one's life. The famous futurist Alvin Toffler in his book "Future Shock" shows that we have a built-in resistance to rapid change. It is safe to say that people resist rapid change – and some resist it with a vengeance.

We feel secure in the things we know. Too much change and too much confrontation with the unknown or the unfamiliar can produce organic and emotional reactions. We see this in the almost suspicious response people have to new trends and fads, and people's feelings can often be overlooked in the response to change, and in the case of rapid change, the normal sensitivities that most people possess seem to vanish as people are so preoccupied with how to cope with the change, feelings are many times overlooked.

Change is a fact of life, particularly where death is concerned.

The changes created by death are a fact of life, but in our day of very rapid change through technological gadgets every hour, to impersonal business decisions, and the endless cycle of exploding knowledge, we are bound to experience exaggerated complications when the normal life is changed when death occurs. In other words, contemporary bereaved people have to modify their ways of living much more significantly than our ancestors ever dreamed of doing.

When death comes, there is bound to be a great and permanent change in human relationships and emotional states. In such turbulent times, it is important to have people around who have stability and dependability. This is one of the hallmark functions of funeral service and funeral professionals. **THIS IS ALSO ONE OF THE REASONS WHY FAMILIES TEND TO ENGAGE THE SAME FUNERAL HOME AND FUNERAL PROFESSIONAL TIME AFTER TIME A DEATH OCCURS.**

It is important to have ways of doing things that are so familiar so that they reduce the emotional effect of too rapid a change. Stable funeral professionals who know how to manage and guide in times of death crises make it possible for the grief-disturbed to stabilize themselves. From this perspective, it is clear that funeral service and funeral professionals contribute indispensably to the mental health of people in their communities.

Familiar ways of doing things not only make it possible to act out deep feelings, but also brings security into life in the very process of acting out those deep feelings. This is why funeral traditions within groups are rarely tampered with. The funeral homes in our towns, villages, and cities provide ways of doing things that people can hold on to when everything else seems to be uncertain and insecure, and funeral professionals are the central providers of guiding the bereaved in wise ways of dealing with changes created by death.

EXAMPLE: "THE NEW FUNERAL DIRECTOR IN TOWN."

One of the most interesting aspects of the funeral service profession is the length of time that some communities take in accepting a new funeral director. This practice, which is very common, is a premier example of how important it is for the bereaved to have something or someone that they know and trust to hold onto.

I remember very well when the "new" funeral director came to town. The funeral home in our community was founded in 1869 (the same year the town was founded). The founder operated the funeral home, furniture store, and ambulance service from 1869-1916, and then his two sons operated the funeral home from 1916 to 1970! In 1970, the youngest brother sold the funeral home when he was 86 years old.

My community was clearly suspicious of the "new funeral director." He did things differently and he was the subject of community gossip and criticism. In time, a level of comfort was attained, but it was not at all unusual for a family to request that the old funeral director (who was now in his nineties) show up for a funeral -and even though he was confined to a wheel chair, some people in our town just wanted the funeral service to be "done right."

Such is the connection of a funeral professional and what they represent in giving people something to hold on to in times of a death crisis.

5. FUNERAL DIRECTORS OFFER PEOPLE SOME THING TO BELIEVE IN

Death challenges our intellects. Death challenges how we live life. Our thoughts and feelings are deep inside us. When events, such as death, cause us strange internal reactions, it is important for us to be able to nourish the structure of the values and thoughts that sustain our life – game playing throughout life just won't accomplish this. For many, this process is synonymous with religious thought.

Even for people who are cynical or who do not affirm a faith, there is an evident need for exploring the meaning of this permanent event, for death can challenge even the most jaded views of life, and death will challenge even the most hardened impersonal and sterile view of life.

For many, death propels them into a type of religious thinking whether they even know it, let alone like it. You often hear people pronounce that "I am not religious, I am spiritual." It is not our purpose here to pick apart this view, however, religious thought does have two cardinal virtues that many people, even jaded people, have found to be helpful when confronted with the stark realities of death. First, all religions acknowledge that life is much more than a mere biological event, and second, that religions acknowledge the existence of the super natural. By offering the idea that the super natural exists, religions offer people interpretations and guidance in exploring the meaning of death in a person's life, which many times leads to deeper spiritual maturity, and greater insights into the character of the person on this grief journey.

We have, for the first time in human history, a scientific framework within which we can view the indestructible energy of consciousness as a practical basis for the ideas of immortality. The nuclear physicist moves beyond sensory measurements of time and space and sees ultimate reality in terms of energy forms that are perceived only with the most delicate instruments. Modern people with a new cosmology and a new psychology can think of their existence with a built-in dimension and this can give them something to believe in, beyond mere physical existence, the presence of the event called death. So, for both the religious and those who are not comfortable with religion or reject it outright, there is something to believe in that can bring security into life in times of death crisis and rapid change. All of these qualities are helpful for those going through the funeral process.

The helper in this process is the funeral professional, and here is an example of how funeral directors give people something to believe in.

CASE STUDY:

One of the most poignant examples of a funeral professional giving people something to believe in is exemplified in this story which I call "The Little Black Book."

Many years ago I worked for a man whom today I call a Great American Funeral Director. This gentleman was one of life's "Unforgettable Characters." He was definitely from the old school in funeral service. His lifelong motto was "families first, no matter what" and he lived this with a consistency that few people ever achieve in attaining their ideals.

The funerals he conducted were flawless and people genuinely admired and respected him. He was a grand person. One of the most interesting aspects of this man was his "little black book." It was a small black book with a lock on the cover. It looked as if it was very old and it was his constant companion.

If you went to his office, you would see it lying on his desk. At funerals, he would pull the black book out and scribble brief notations in it. He wouldn't do this all the time, just once in a while.

If you picked up his suit coat, you could feel the black book in his coat pocket.

Can you just imagine the gossip and speculation around the funeral home coffee room by the staff as to what was in the black book? I remember the first day I worked for him, the embalmer told me to be on the lookout for the little black book. Soon enough, I saw him take it out and scribble in it. Later that day, I asked the embalmer what the book was for, and he responded with a very knowing glance, "Well, what do you think is in the book?" I was not the sharpest knife in the drawer and very innocently said, "I have no idea." "Oh, come on farm boy," the embalmer replied. "He keeps his list of girlfriends in there." I was stunned!

Later I asked the receptionist about the black book, her response was that it was where he kept the list of the horses he bet on at the race track. Again, I was stunned. My employer was a womanizing horse better! I could not believe it.

For nearly three years the mysterious saga of the little black book continued. All the time, the stories, gossip, and intrigue getting more and more spectacular and ridiculous.

Then suddenly one day, while conducting a funeral, my boss, this great funeral director, died. He had a massive heart attack just as we were putting the casket in the funeral coach and was dead when he hit the ground. I was crushed.

Four days later, we had a grand funeral for him. He was laid out in a solid bronze casket, flowers were everywhere and when we took him to the church, the place was packed and the Governor of the State was in the front row.

I was standing in the back of the church with the church truck (that was my job), as the minister went on about what a great man my boss was and how just knowing him made us all better people. I couldn't have agreed with the minister more.

Then the minister asked my boss's widow to come up and talk about her husband's character. I thought, "Now this will be great," as she rose to walk to the pulpit. It was then I saw she was carrying his little black book! My tears of grief instantaneously turned to sweats of terror. "Gosh almighty, "I thought, "What will she say, Oh, what does she know?"

She walked to the pulpit, stood with complete dignity and looked at the assembly and said, "Thank you all for being here today. I want to share with you a secret about my husband's character." I thought, "Oh boy, here it comes!" She continued, "You see this small book. Most of you know he carried it with him constantly. I would like to read to you the first entry of the book dated April 17, 1920 - Mary Flannery she is all alone. The next entry August 8, 1920 - Fred Pritchard, he is all alone. The next entry – Edna Gale November 15, 1920, she is all alone.

You see, when he made funeral arrangements with somebody that he knew would now be all alone because of the death, he would write their name in this book. Then at Christmas time he would call each person, maybe only three or four people a year, and invite them to share a wonderful Christmas dinner at our house.

I want you to know that this was the true character of my husband; he was concerned, compassionate, and caring. This is what the little black book is all about, and I also want you to know that this being 1971, he did this for 56 Christmases."

There was not a dry eye in the church, and I remember thinking, "I knew that book wasn't a book of women or horses!"

Now many years after his death, I look back at the inner spirit that motivated this funeral director to do what he did. During his life he truly gave people, humble ordinary everyday people something to believe in.

May this belief in kind, thoughtful, and compassionate action guide each of us in our work in this great profession. Just think of the believing in others possibilities if every member of the funeral profession developed their own little black books. The results of believing in human kindness and acting on it would be staggering!

ASSESSMENT

We began this chapter by asking the most difficult question a human being can ask oneself is "Who Am I and/or Who Am I to be Counseling?" While this question is difficult, it need not be. To be sure the process of answering it can sometimes be painful, it is nonetheless ultimately required of every funeral professional who genuinely loves our great profession to ask.

Take time, every day, to ask this all important question. Your answers will help you improve your skills as a human being and as a funeral professional. And when we as funeral professionals improve our care of our families we serve, we will automatically improve, and this is a very admirable life goal.

As we move into our next areas of exploration the remaining information will build upon the five inner resources that everyone in our beloved profession already possess.

THE WISDOM AND LOGIC OF FUNERAL COUNSELING

A first principle in funeral service counseling is that helping the bereaved comes not only from what is said, but also from what is done.

The activities of the funeral are one of the most accessible and economical form of grief help available to everyone. It is an individually oriented process that starts with the death and culminates with the final disposition of the body and continues with aftercare to the living. This process is called the "Cycle of Service."

The funeral has its own built-in wisdom and logic for it responds to the need for people to go through a series of meaningful events that satisfy their deep needs. Whenever we study the ceremonies surrounding death, whether in primitive culture or in modern society, we find this innate wisdom at work to satisfy the emotional needs of persons faced with the acute crises that death creates.

Paramount to the internal wisdom of funeral counseling is the social purposes and values of the funeral. In its most elementary form all funerals are a social function. Said another way, it is terribly difficult to have a funeral without people as wise procedures, wise insights, and wise counsel is the exclusive province of human beings. As crazy as this might sound, people cannot obtain wise insights from animals, this can only be had by connections with other human beings.

THE SOCIAL PURPOSES OF THE FUNERAL

The funeral in its purest form is usually a public ritual to which all are invited and none are excluded. Socially, funerals serve a three valid purposes, and each one involves human beings:

1. They give all in the community a chance to share in the grief work.
2. They meet the acute needs of those who are in a state of emotional crises.
3. They give the general public a chance to do any unfinished grief work.

Because of this three-fold, validity based inherent nature of the ancient wisdom of the funeral, the private funeral is truly a denial of the social wisdom lessons which generations of human being have learned from participating in funeral rituals and ceremonies. The effort to deal with death privately rejects the ancient wisdom that acknowledges the importance of the concern and support of the community. The private funeral violates the wisdom of the centuries, and in the end, the consequences as it deliberately or accidentally excludes and rejects most of the wise and therapeutic psychological aspects of the funeral process.

THE SIX LOGICAL STEPS OF THE FUNERAL

The funeral involves at least logical six steps that need to be accepted and implemented in proper order. When this order is violated, ignored, or denied, there is apt to be a denial and forfeiture of the basic resources that the value of the funeral affords. These six steps are:

1. The event of the death.
2. The notification of the event of death.
3. The confrontation of the reality of the death.
4. The inclusive support of the community.
5. The providing of religion, spiritual and/or philosophical support.
6. The farewell ritual for the decedent.

1. THE EVENT OF DEATH

The event of death is the starting point for the series of time limited events that characterize the funeral. Naturally, the death comes first.

2. THE NOTIFICATION OF THE EVENT

The notification of the event of death is an important part of the process of summoning family and community to participate in the funeral process. The family and friends and general community have a right to know of a death so that they can respond accordingly. This leads to the confrontation of the reality of the death. If, however, the confrontation precedes the notification, it can be traumatic.

When there is notification before the death or confusion surrounding the notification, a variety of embarrassing and interesting circumstances can develop.

This happened in the life of Alfred Nobel, the inventor of dynamite. The press published his obituary prematurely and wrote that the man whose invention had killed thousands (dynamite in bombs) had died himself. Mr. Nobel read the brutal reports of his life and death with horror and when he tried to correct the error, it caused people to feel uncomfortable, embarrassed and at a loss for words as how to respond properly – it was not humorous. It was one gigantic mess! When there is in reality no death, it is inappropriate, distressing, and unfortunate as well as inaccurate. When this happens from the start, this logical proper order is violated and the normal progressive nature of the funeral process is disturbed.

Interestingly, Mr. Nobel was motivated by reading the scathing notices of his death that he resolved that the world would not remember him for inventing something that killed thousands of people. Hence, Mr. Nobel, who was independently wealthy started a philanthropic organization known today as the Nobel Prize. The Nobel Prize is today given to people who are humanitarians of the first order, and whose work on behalf of the human race has made the world a much better place.

CASE STUDY:

This occurred in my funeral career. In 1975, a father called me and asked for advice and counsel concerning his daughter who had gone through the tragic experience of confrontation with death before notification.

She was attending college many miles away and had been riding one evening with a young man she was dating. They saw a car with motor trouble, stopped and the man got out of the car to inquire as to how they might be of help. When he turned back into the road, he was hit by a car traveling at high speed and was hurled a hundred and forty feet into a field. Death was instantaneous. The young woman frantically left her car and searched the field, in darkness, until she stumbled over his body in deep grass. The impact of this tragic moment of discovery deeply disturbed her.

The logical order of the funeral process was disrupted by circumstances, that truly were beyond anyone's control had turned into a psychologically harrowing experience with years of haunting memories, as the result.

As dramatic as this case study is, it is non-the-less the exception. Most people do not die this way, the point being that most people die with the opportunity for the logical sequence of notification to take place, and this is an extremely important portion of the entire funeral experience. To be sure, sometimes we have no control in these types of circumstances, but truth is most time we do, and we should take advantage of proper notification.

In the end, the logic of proper notification gives the chance for tentative exploration of the deep feelings of loss that are involved. This may at first involve denial, but it should engage the person in the orderly process of moving toward confrontation and then on through the other steps that are essential parts of the funeral process.

3. THE CONFRONTATION OF REALITY

This involves honest confrontation with what has happened, many times this is referred to as "establishing the reality of death".

Honest confrontation with what has really happened is important to break through the natural defenses which include denial and the desire to run away from the painful reality. ***In fact, Dr. Erich Lindemann (the Harvard professor and author of "The Coconut Grove Fire Study") contended that this was the most important part of the whole funeral process, for when the living person confronts the dead body, he or she is compelled to break through any denials and come to terms with reality.***

The decedent is the ultimate symbol of death's final and permanent reality. It is a moment of truth that helps to marshal the inner resources essential to meet the deep inner needs to cope with loss.

Establishing the reality of death is most often the beginning point of the healing process for the bereaved. It is tremendously difficult for many to face up to this, but in the long run this essential wisdom inherent in the logical process of the funeral is very important. It should not be underestimated concerning its value and worth.

Yet there are people who seem to feel otherwise. They chant the repeated line "I would rather remember them when they were alive." However catchy as these words may be, people who hide behind them offer little support for this position other than, denial, humor, anxieties and sarcasm. It sounds good, but it is not good!

This approach to the reality of death is an ineffectual coping mechanism. People who advocate avoiding the painful task of facing reality appear to feel that they may in some mysterious or clever way avoid the pain of grief and the need to process mourning – this is a coping mechanism, but it is a poor coping mechanism.

"I would rather remember them when they were alive" is a poor coping mechanism because it is dishonest. The dead person is NOT alive. This never really works, it is just an illusion of convenience. Another catchy phrase is "No funeral, no grief ' may be attractive to people fearful of confronting honestly the reality of death, but the idea is full of perilous psychological traps.

The way our feelings work, we do not have these simplistic and immature forms of choice that seem to be so neatly tied up in our catchy contemporary phraseologies.

We do not decide whether or not we will have a painful experience at the time of loss. The only choice we have is whether or not we will manage the loss so that we have a clean wound that can heal quickly, or whether we will have an infected wound that will heal slowly and with great difficulty. It seems to be a valid psychological observation that the more quickly and the more honestly a person confronts the fact and reality of death, the more quickly the process of rebuilding the inner being and resources will take place.

Naturally, as professionals want us the grieving people, who seek our guidance and help, to do the right thing AND SO WE WOULD NOT, AS FUNERAL PROFESSIONALS, encourage them or conspire with them to do things that violate their own best interest. Would we? Hence, I firmly recommend viewing the remains, so the bereaved might logically and emotionally experience the ultimate psychological benefits in confrontation with death.

CASE STUDY:

Several years ago I was privileged to visit the United States Mortuary at Hickam Air Force Base in Honolulu, Hawaii.

The facilities and people were first class, and one left the experience with the unmistakable knowledge that the government of the United States believes in, endorses, and practices the ethic of reverence for the dead.

During the tour, I had an experience that literally reconfirmed for me, the importance of the work the funeral profession does to help the mental health of communities by establishing the reality of death, and by bringing formal closure to life through rites, rituals, and ceremonies.

While I was walking through the military mortuary facility, I eventually ended up on the place where the Missing in Action soldiers are identified. This room was quite large, and on numerous tables there were hundreds of bones with anthropologists trying to unravel the mystery of who these people were in life.

I struck up a conversation with one of the anthropologists, and she told me about the value of saying goodbye, establishing the reality of death, the value, benefit and purpose of funeral rituals and bringing some closure to one of life's major events - the death of someone we are attached to.

Our conversation revolved around the identification of a U.S. service man who had been dead and missing for fifty-one years. The body was positively identified at the military mortuary, and this deceased man's mother was still alive and living in Pennsylvania.

Proper notification was made, and the mother's instructions were to bring her son back home for burial. The bones of the man were placed in a plastic body pouch, the uniform of his rank laid over the pouch, this was then placed in a military casket, and the casket was draped with the national colors.

An Air Force transport flew the body to San Francisco and then on to Pennsylvania. The anthropologist went as an escort.

The anthropologist said that at the calling hours at the funeral home, the mother sat close by the head of the casket patting the casket and rubbing the flag on her cheek throughout the evening. The mother, the anthropologist thought, expressed her deep attachment to her son by this activity.

Interestingly, the mother of the deceased ignored the anthropologist throughout all of the funeral rituals until they took the sacred remains to the cemetery for final consignment.

At the burial the next day, the military performed their customary ritual and presented this man's mother with the flag which covered his casket.

Following the committal, the mother finally approached the anthropologist and asked, "The undertaker tells me you are the person who identified my son?" The military anthropologist answered, "Yes, I am." With that, the mother's eyes welled up with tears, and she said, "My dear, I want to thank you from the bottom of my heart. Do you know what it is like not to sleep for fifty-one years? I worried about him so much, was he alive or dead? If he was alive, why can't he get home, and if he is dead why can't they bring him home? They finally brought him home, and you know tonight I will finally sleep, tonight I know where my baby is."

The anthropologist was overwhelmed by this experience, and she relayed to me that at that moment she became committed to the value, benefit and purpose of the funeral, and in the therapeutic value of confronting reality of death no matter how long it had been since the event of loss.

4. <u>GROUP SUPPORT</u>

In times of crisis our social nature tends to reach out to others for group support. With this reach often times comes understanding, love, confirmation and support. Quite simply put, in times of crisis, many of us need human help and we can usually get it from other humans (this seems clearly to be the mission of the funeral profession).

Funeral help normally provides both formal and informal ways by which group support can be provided. A wake, visitation, calling hours, Shiva and times of sharing provides a very important time and place where people can meet, talk, and share their feelings. The more formal services also provide the opportunity for neighbors, friends, and the community to come together to provide this supportive relationship.

From this perspective then, the obituary is not a mere news announcement placed in the classified ads, but rather a serious call for support by grieving people. Most funeral professionals can attest to the critical importance of the proper placement and timing of the obituary, for if the obituary is wrong or worse is not even published the consequences for most every funeral professional on earth will be very unpleasant!

The informal funeral help from people may vary from place to place, but it usually involves gift-giving and gift-receiving. Whether it be a salad, a cake, a book, or flowers the intent is the same.

Flowers are the most ancient type of funeral gift and speak an eloquent, though non-verbal language. In many ways, the human community gathers around the emotionally wounded and seeks to give them strength to face the painful reality, as well as the assurance that their deep feelings are understood and accepted for what they are, the manifestations of a love or friendship that is fractured.

This social support by the group for the bereaved is one of the primary reasons that funeral homes even exist. The funeral home is the place where the isolation of the bereaved is liberated and the bereaved can be shown attention without invading the privacy of their own home.

CASE STUDY:

In 1974, the father of two maiden sisters died and I was called to handle the funeral. The father was 102 years old and his two daughters were 78 and 80 years old. The two sisters had not spoken to each other since 1918 at the end of World War I. They had lived in the same town, only three blocks apart, but had not uttered one syllable to each other for fifty-six years. Everyone in town knew of their distance, but no one knew the real story.

The older sister had nursed the father throughout a lingering illness until his death. This sister took complete control of the funeral and requested that her sister's name be left out of the obituary. No amount of compassionate persuasion could change her mind and the obituary when printed listed only the elder daughter as the survivor.

We laid the father in the chapel and the elder daughter gave her blessing to the work we had done. There would be two days of calling hours and a funeral on the third day.

At three o'clock on the second day, the elder sister sat alone in the chapel when the younger sister came through the front door. The younger sister had a small black jewelry case and walked right over to her elder sister and said very bluntly, "This really belongs to you, I am sorry for keeping it so long, but I was jealous when Papa gave it to you - here take this and with it my apology, for what it is worth."

The elder sister sat down took the black jewelry case, opened it up, and sobbed for an hour, all the time embracing and kissing her younger sister. It was a touching and valuable moment, and none of us knew what was actually going on.

Only later, we learned that when the father had returned to the states after the war, he gave his elder daughter a military hero medal that General John J. Pershing had given him. One day in a fit of jealousy, the youngest daughter stole the medal but tried to convince the eldest daughter that it was just lost and would turn up someday. Of course the eldest daughter did not believe the story and hence a fifty-six year feud ensued.

There had been the event of death, a proper notification, and even the establishment of the reality of death, but it took another of the logical sequence of the wisdom of the funeral, namely group support, for this to happen. I question seriously if such healing would ever had taken place had not the funeral home had its doors opened, and available so emotions could be expressed. If the sisters hadn't been in the environment of the funeral home would this have happened anyway? Possibly, but remember friends they had lived only blocks away for over a half a century and nothing had taken place. The wisdom and logic of the funeral ritual is an unspoken motivator for the drama of human life to unfold – its potentials are truly limitless.

Such are the social possibilities of relationship healing through the funeral and the purpose of funeral home. I doubt very much whether this resolution of love and justice would have occurred in any place other than the funeral home under the circumstances; the funeral home was indeed the appropriate atmosphere to stimulate such behavior.

5. **RELIGIOUS, SPIRITUAL AND PHILOSOPHICAL SUPPORT**

One aspect of the funeral process is so important that it deserves special attention. After a person has gone through the process of confronting the reality of death, and having that reality confirmed by themselves and the community, there is a need to move on from the confrontation of death to the confrontation of life and the resources for continued living.

The manner in which people process this movement varies widely. For instance, some people turn to drugs and alcohol as their resources for confronting life, others turn to the profession of psychiatric care, some turn on themselves and self-destruct through suicide, and others freeze their emotional growth for the rest of their lives, and hence, are isolated and immune from both the joys and sorrows that life has in store.

For many though, religion has become the resource for coping wisely from a loss that is experienced, and this seems to have a great deal of wisdom behind it. Religion affirms first that the fact of life is more than a biological function. It has tried to assure people that there is something about the human that is more than a physical body, and that the supernatural exists and within that invisible realm hope of eternity is a reality.

For many, even avid anti-religious people, when they suffer a loss, they experience a need to experience a larger perspective on life because they have been thrust into a larger than life experience. The former Surgeon General C. Everett Koop summed this idea up very well when he wrote that "there are no atheists at the bedside of a dying child."

What Dr. Koop meant was this: death challenges most of our security and stability resources. When people die, oftentimes even for the unreligious, religious type thinking is stimulated whether the person labels it as religious or not.

Hence, what religious thought has to offer in the funeral and in the experience of funeral counseling is of great importance. In fact, this unique period of time of facing grief, stimulating faith, and gaining the larger perspective is so important that every effort should be made in funeral counseling to aid the religious officiant in her or his significant task. The importance of this issue is so evident that today funeral professionals are taking on the role of "surrogate" ministers by default of simply being present. Add to this that the "celebrant" movement has become ever more popular in our profession, and this alone affirms the ancient need for the bereaved to find ways to express their feelings.

Even when people deny a specific form of religious faith, the psychological equivalent (celebrant services) should be provided by some form of service that puts the tragic events of life into a larger cosmic pattern.

Action upon emotions should provide some of the important values that are usually found in the religious service, even if the word religious is never mentioned. It is important to remember from a funeral service counseling perspective that just because people may not be religious in the strict sense, is not a reason for denying them the resources that are a part of spiritual and meditative growth. Regardless of the form, the funeral needs to be designed around the following guidelines:

- The funeral ritual should be instructive. It has a teaching role which is limitless.
- The funeral ritual should indoctrinate people. Not indoctrination akin to brain-washing, but instead it is an opportunity to share belief systems. Indoctrination usually includes suggestions on avenues of help that the bereaved might well have never thought about before.
- The funeral should interpret events. It should explain why the loss has happened and the need to confront reality with honesty.

6. FAREWELL RITUAL FOR THE DECEDENT AND THE LIVING: FINAL CONSIGNMENT

Last, but certainly not least, is the farewell, taking the decedent through internment, cremation, or removal to a medical school for gross anatomical dissection. To leave a body without an accepted farewell is unsanitary, unlawful, and uncaring. There is a finality and completeness about this act of final farewell that is both symbolic and essential. Persons who have avoided this part of the funeral have reported to me that they have a feeling of incompleteness and amazingly these innocent people wonder why.

There is no life without death and vice versa. All that we are physically comes from the earth, and it is appropriate that the physical forms in which we have lived are returned to the earth either bodily or as cremated remains. Symbolically, what falls to the earth has a way of springing up into new life. We plant seeds with the hope of new growth. The meaning of this final farewell ritual, and visually completing this part of the funeral process may be of great importance to those who have suffered loss.

Taking on the responsibility of fulfilling the principles of funeral counseling means never ignoring this critical step or underestimating its importance in the logical sequence of the healing nature of the funeral ritual.

CASE STUDY: "THE FOOTBALL TEAM"

In the mid 1970's, a young man who was the star of the high school football team in our community was tragically killed in an automobile accident. The person killed was 17 years old, came from a well-respected family, and was a good student.

Any funeral professional reading this case study can well imagine the explosion of grief reactions from the entire community and particularly the students and faculty of the high school.

Adolescent grief is a highly intense and volatile and thespian experience.

The six logical steps that I have already outlined here were indeed taking place, but it was at the cemetery, at the final farewell ritual that one could visually see that the members of his football team were in a particularly distressing situation.

These young men were at a loss as how to wisely express their grief. While the logical six steps had been valuable and effective for most of the community and bereaved family it was clear, even at the funeral home calling hours, that this important group of people were lost. They clearly didn't know how to express their emotions, as they simply stood around the lobby of the funeral home with their hands in their pockets, saying appropriate but stupid comments for teenagers, laughing at the wrong time, and just grunting when someone would try to engage any of them in conversation.

Most of these young men were extremely large in size and had already learned very well how to behave like "macho men."

Later nervousness, irritability, and insomnia were words used by the parents of these team members to describe their behavior, before they all went to participate in the final farewell ritual.

This internal tension was actually innocent grief ignorance which was awkwardly trying to find a way to express itself, but unfortunately, the first five steps of the funeral process failed to accommodate this pressing need.

We went in procession to the cemetery for the final farewell service. At the conclusion of the committal service the other mourners in turn left to go home, but the members of this football team lingered. They would not or could not leave the grave. Finally, by pure chance, I asked the young men if they would like to help the sexton fill in the grave. Immediately, they all responded with great interest and enthusiasm. The sexton also supported this idea (less work for him, understandably) and went to the shed get several more shovels.

These boys took off their jackets and began to work; and work they did! The dirt was flying everywhere; the boys were sweating profusely; and you could literally see the tension of their unresolved grief begin to disappear.

One hour later, the work was completed. Exhausted and covered with dirt and sweat these young men, now had a totally different mental attitude. They left the cemetery with the feeling that they had participated in their friend's final farewell and hence, they had done the right thing. Also, they had literally worked off much of their internal stress by using large muscle activity. This is the exact same principle as when someone jogs or exercises to relieve stress.

Later, the parents reported to me that their sons slept the sleep of the saved and innocent after they had participated in this valuable activity in the funeral process. I have often pondered how these young men would have fared had not the opportunity to participate in the final disposition of their good friend been afforded them? As with the two old spinster sisters who finally reconciled in the funeral home, even though they only lived block away from each other, this final logical step of farewell was afforded by the funeral – yes it might have happened somewhere else, in some other fashion, but they we will never know the answer to those *questions, will we? What we know is that within the six logical steps of the ancient ritual we call the funeral lurks possibilities for grief help that people can only experience if they have a funeral and participate in the six logical steps.*

OBJECTIVES IN FUNERAL COUNSELING

Within the structure of funeral service counseling, there are four major objectives. They are:

1. The need to face reality.
2. The need to express feelings.
3. The need for group support.
4. The need to develop inner resources.

1. THE NEED TO FACE REALITY

Under stress, people try to avoid pain and discomfort. With physical pain we can faint. With emotional pain we can try to deny the reality which is distressing. In effect, we try to convince ourselves that it really isn't so. Some people even go so far as to think that if they have no funeral, in some magic or carefree way they can avoid the pain of death and grief. Quite the opposite is true. Denial spreads the crisis all through life and makes it even harder to manage it wisely. It is always more sound to face the facts no matter how difficult and reject the falsehood of denial. The things people do at the time of death help them face reality fully and completely. Only then are they in a position to healthfully work through the crisis. Illusion and delusion are components of emotional illness. An honest recognition of reality moves people toward emotional health.

CASE STUDY: "MARY"

I was called by Mary in 1979 to care for her mother's funeral. It was the first funeral that Mary had ever attended. Mary's mother had taken her own life. Mary had grown up in a family that protected children from death and evoked a great amount of death anxiety. Three of her grandparents had died when she was a child, but she did not attend the funerals.

Mary's other grandparent died in Florida when she was thirty-five. At this time, Mary was living in California and had just had a baby. Her parents strongly objected to her attending the funeral of the last grandparent. Mary's mother assured her that the grandparent would want everyone to remember her as she was alive. Mary did not attend the last grandparent's funeral.

When Mary's own mother died, she arranged a disposition with me that reflected her lifelong avoidance of death. Nothing I said in funeral counseling had any effect (this sometimes happens). Mary never saw her mother's corpse - and neither did anyone else. She insisted the casket be kept closed.

She later she told me that she was never totally convinced her mother was in it.

Years later, she relayed how she experienced frequent dream states where she received a telegram announcing that her dead mother had *"finally been located"* and that the report of the suicide was incorrect. Then she would awake from those dreams panicked, hopeful, and confused. Then, as reality took over, she was overwhelmed by a rush of pain as raw and all consuming as it was on the day her mother had died.

Mary's difficulty originated in her systematic avoidance of the reality of her situations. Mary lived in a world of delusion that death had nothing to do with her, even when the event of death was intimately staring her in the face.

In effect, Mary spent years re-burying her mother through confusing dream states. In her effort to shelter herself and others from pain, she left open an emotional door which took her years to close.

When Mary's mother-in-law died seven years later, she availed the resources of the funeral to face reality and viewed the dead human body, availed the six logical steps, and had a healthy final farewell at the crematory.

2. THE NEED TO EXPRESS FEELINGS

Feelings have their own validity – people constantly try, but in truth no one can tell you how to feel. They are a valid part of us and cannot be compared or measured. We do not decide whether or not we are going to have feelings. All we can do is decide whether or not we are going to respect them and express them wisely. We have a tendency to feel uncomfortable in the presence of strong feelings. We may try to keep people from crying. This is unwise, for nature's safety valves have a purpose, and it is better to express feelings than to repress them.

CASE STUDY: *It has often crossed my mind when I speak to younger funeral directors about the period of time that we operated the ambulance service how much they missed concerning learning about the raw data stuff of life.*

Here is an experience that I had years ago when I innocently witnessed how allied professionals can unwittingly conspire to sacrifice a person's knowledge of grief's meaning and reality on the altar of their own anxieties.

When I was a student in Boston, we received an ambulance call one afternoon where a construction worker had suffered a terrible accident where his left leg had been amputated.

This was years before the days of Emergency Medical Technicians and paramedics. What we offered was as sophisticated treatment as was possible at the time - Advanced First Aid. When we arrived at the scene, it was clear to most that the man was already dead, but the instructions from the State Police was to transport him to the hospital where he would be pronounced "Dead on Arrival."

In the meantime, while all the activity was taking place at the accident scene, the State Police had notified the man's wife and told her that we were in route to the hospital. The wife was not told that her husband was, in fact, already dead.

The timing was unbelievable. Just as we pulled into the ambulance entrance, the wife pulled up right behind the ambulance. No one actually realized who she was until she started screaming when we pulled her husband's body out of the back of the ambulance. There is no need to graphically describe what this scene looked like.

The wife followed us into the hospital and the following scenario was unfortunately played out. As the wife screamed and sobbed, the emergency room physician came out and pointed to her and said, "Get her the hell out of here!" A nurse came over and said, "Now, we can't have this here," and the chaplain came over and told her that for her own good she should return to her car until she could calm down because she was disturbing the other patients and staff. With this remark, the wife picked up a ceramic lamp and threw it across the waiting room. The hospital called security and she was escorted from the facility.

Now, this happened many years ago, and things have changed in many favorable ways as to how opportunities for the bereaved to express feelings is handled. The significance of this case study, however, is to ask for a close examination of our own attitudes towards loss and the development a healthy, sensitive and insightful appreciation of the needs of others to express their grief.

3. THE NEED FOR GROUP SUPPORT

We are social beings. Our language, our culture, our structure of relationships emanates from group processes. During the crises of life, we seek the understanding and response of those around us. In funeral service, this process takes the form of a wake, visitation, Shiva, or time of sharing. People affected by a death want to know what has happened and also to accept and share feelings. No one can be a complete person without fruitful relationships with others. No one can cope well with the major crises of life in isolation. Because of this, public sharing of the death experience is important because it is not safe to draw lines as to who is affected and who is not by a death. For this reason private funerals have identifiable limitations. So it is of great importance for people to be able to relate effectively and communicate meaningfully when they are in times of stress. This process of communication can take place formally or informally, through the funeral experience with family, neighbors, and friends.

CASE STUDY: *In 1974, I made funeral arrangements with a man whose wife had died very suddenly. Throughout the arrangement conference, the bereaved husband was extremely agitated. He demanded absolute control, was supremely self-confident, but at the same time was almost in a panic state.*

He had four children, but allowed none of them to attend the conference. He was about sixty years old and was financially successful.

Upon sitting down, he immediately gave me the following orders in almost a military style. First, he wanted the body of his wife disposed of immediately - no matter what method of disposition, he wanted it done in the quickest fashion possible, even if it would cost more! Second, he was set on the fact that he did not want any people "parading around" (to use his exact phrase), or snooping around his home or the funeral home "fiddling" (to use his exact word) with his private business. He wanted to be alone so he refused all my suggestions concerning a public obituary.

The arrangement conference lasted thirty minutes and he made it clear that he wanted no assistance from me or the funeral home. The legal and business papers were signed and the formalities were completed.

Three weeks later, this same bereaved husband came to the funeral home to settle the expenses. Now, however, he had a totally different appearance. Whereas before he was an agitated ball of fire, barking orders, demanding his privacy even from his children. He was now actually so extremely sad. He stared at his shoelaces while I prepared the paperwork.

Finally, he looked at me in tears and said, "Boy, you sure know who your friends are when you get in a pinch." "How so?" I implied. "You know not one of my neighbors came over, called, wrote or anything after my wife died!" "How could they all ignore me like that?"

Without damaging his self-esteem, I suggested that now he might place an obituary in the newspaper and that this would help open the door for the type of group support that he so desperately needed.

4. THE NEED TO DEVELOP INNER RESOURCES

There is a human need to discover and develop the inner resources that can help a person through an emotional crisis. As external events produce internal crisis, so also the resources for resolving the external crisis must be developed from within. Of course, there can be help from those around the bereaved person. And because most times the funeral professional is on the scene we play an indispensable role.

But if there is to be a healthful resolving of life's crises, the inner being must be strong or must develop strength. These inner resources can come through reason, group support, personal insight, and perception on the events of life. The initial response to crises or threats to the security system of the individual usually triggers the basic defense mechanisms of the person. No one can live continually with his or her defenses up. One must learn to build bridges from his or her initial emotional response to more calm and reasoned judgements.

The alternatives certainly possess negative consequences. Only by so doing can one move into the future with the ability to manage life. Discovering the resources for this type of wise self-management is of great importance.

For this precise reason, in funeral counseling aftercare programs and attempts take on an even more significant role.

CASE STUDY: *In my early years of preparing to become a funeral director, I witnessed this happen in the funeral home I worked at.*

We were called to handle the funeral of an eight year old girl who had contracted meningitis and had died a painful and debilitating death. Her parents had long since abandoned her and she had lived with her maternal grandparents. The family had moved from Mexico to our community where the grandfather had retired from the railroad. The grandparents and the granddaughter were devote Roman Catholics.

The preparation of the deceased proceeded very carefully and when the funeral arrangements were made, the grandparents honestly told my employer that because of legal troubles with the girl's parents, they were low on funds. They were highly relieved when they learned that our funeral home had a longstanding policy not to charge for the funerals of children.

A white child's casket was delivered, the body casketed and the symbols of mourning of the Church appropriately displayed.

At 10:30 a.m. the door-bell rang at the funeral home and the grandfather was standing on the porch. It was clear he had been drinking. He asked me if he could come in and spend some time with his "Baby" as he called her. The old man staggered into the Chapel and began to weep and sob. He did not stop for two hours. By 1:00 p.m. I could see that between the alcohol and crying he had exhausted himself. I asked him if he wanted a bite to eat and he said no. A half an hour later, I went to check on him and found him sound asleep on the floor next to the casket. I shut the doors of the Chapel and let him sleep. Formal calling hours were not to begin until the next day.

I was making this all up as I went, and I was scared to death!

At 6:30 p.m., five hours later, the doors to the Chapel opened and the grandfather was a new man. He had wept himself dry, and slept off the alcohol and stress, and sat with me for another hour talking about his granddaughter. When he left the funeral home, he turned around and said to me, "I will be alright."

You could see the man muster all his inner resources to get through this "valley of death" before your eyes - and he was alright. He had dealt with his shadows and continued to live a fruitful life.

This is yet another example of the influence of funeral service counseling. It is also a prime example that one, funeral service counseling does not have to be confined to the arrangement office of the funeral home, and two, that our working definition that counseling is anytime anybody helps someone with a problem is highly applicable to our profession – in fact, this case study shows that counseling happens all the time in every funeral home whether anybody calls it counseling or not!

THE CHALLENGES OF FUNERAL COUNSELING

UNPOPULAR SUBJECTS

Because I am highly committed to funeral service and out of a deep love for the good funeral service does, I am compelled to sum up this glaring challenge of funeral counseling this way: ***the subjects of death and funerals are not, have never, and probably will never ever be popular or even interesting to many people.*** Herein lies the challenge that faces every funeral professional in the world: the death rate is 100% and people are not comfortable with the subject or that fact.

Given this combination it is no wonder that many people are on a collision course with the inevitable and poorly prepared both emotionally and situationally. It then becomes of great importance and significant as to how the funeral professionals handle this awkward and stressful situation.

When people are anxious and fearful about death, they usually think it is going to be very difficult to talk with someone about it, and as most funeral professionals can attest, it many times the case. ***BUT THE ESSENTIAL FACT OF FUNERAL SERVICE COUNSELING IS THE FACT THAT IN TIMES OF GREAT NEED PEOPLE CAN AND DO RESPOND WELL TO THOSE IN FUNERAL SERVICE WHO REALLY TRY TO HELP THEM.***

Time and again people who have a loss enter a funeral counseling relationship feeling that it will be a great difficulty, but time after time, end up replacing those initial feeling of difficulty with confidence and genuine appreciation of the relationship they have built with the funeral professional through the counseling or helping process.

It is important that to understand the challenge of funeral counseling we respect and appreciate the magnitude and utter complexity of how people die. This statement seems to be true: there is only one way to be born, but there are a million ways to die. All death experiences are different and hence, not all death is experienced the same way. To help us organize this complex subject, we can systematize the differences of degree and emotional response to death by categorizing death in two different ways. Each of these categories has its own particular set of feelings that as funeral counselors we need to be aware of.

EXPECTED NATURAL DEATH

Natural, timely death is most common. Nearly 70% of all deaths occur among people who have lived a full number of years. Here the element of acute tragedy is often times ameliorated because death is more appropriate for the aged; however, this may not always be true and it is risky to make black and white comments concerning death.

Regardless, it is safe to say that if a person lives long enough, a process of slow physical deterioration takes place which is clearly visible. Strength wanes and vitality slips away. For the survivors, a long period of anticipating grief may be involved and so the person had a chance to prepare for the inevitable event.

While sadness may exit, it is not so apt to be acute and the funeral process is entered into with a minimum of distress and a maximum of preparation.

With natural death, the funeral counseling process is less complicated. It provides the opportunity to act out the feelings appropriately and use the funeral as a final farewell ceremony on a life that has completed its natural course. All funerals are highly important, but in this death situation what is needed is a ceremony that offers group support, creates a climate for expressing feelings and offers the important chance to face the reality of the event. For the death of an older person, it is most important to include children in the event so they begin to experience the learning elements of the cycle of life - the alpha to the omega.

UNNATURAL, UNEXPECTED, UNTIMELY DEATH

Unnatural, untimely, or unexpected death is usually more devastating to the survivors because they have had no chance to prepare, take a defensive stance nor do anticipatory grief work. These persons who suffer from acute grief are apt to retreat from the painful reality into denial. At first, they may want to avoid all funeral experiences as if to say that by denial of death they will be spared the painful feelings of grief. This is not only unsatisfactory as far as facing reality is concerned, but in the long run it may be definitely damaging - for it prevents the working through of deep feelings and may produce physical, mental and emotional illness.

With the people who have experienced the acute grief that comes with tragic suddenness, it is important to provide extra opportunities for group support, more time for talking out the deep feelings and added opportunities for facing the meaning of the highly significant events that have occurred. Instead of having fewer rites, rituals and ceremonies it is critical to have as many and as varied opportunities for acting out grief as possible. Instead of side stepping the six logical steps, now the wisdom of following them step by step is greatly magnified, and the avoidance of the logical steps has greatly magnified consequences.

The more these six logical steps are suggested by the funeral professional at the beginning, the more readily the person usually undertakes the painful but necessary task of withdrawing his or her emotional capital from the loved decedent so he or she can get on with the important task of healing and living.

DIAGNOSIS AND AFTERCARE

DIAGNOSIS

Diagnosis is the province of the physician, the specialist in emotional and physical disorders. Funeral professionals do not want to set themselves up as diagnosticians. However, as funeral professionals, we are people first, and we all know very well that as people we all perform functions that come close to diagnosis at times.

If your child is ill you decide whether or not the condition requires a doctor - you make a practical diagnosis on the way toward a more precise evaluation. If you slip and fall, you must decide whether it is serious enough to call a doctor or whether it is just a bruise that will take care of itself.

When you are dealing with people in the death crisis situation, you will often times see signs of distress and other evidence of what we call grief. This is usually a time relative modification of behavior that is clearly related to the observed cause, namely the loss of someone or something of significance. Here, the person usually rights themselves in time.

EXCESSIVE BEHAVIOR

It is when the person has serious deviation from the normal course of grieving that we need to show special concern. If a person is not able to function, he or she needs special help. If they are excessively hostile, dependent, suspicious or anxious, these are danger signals. But the key word is excessively! Again it is important to realize that there are differences in people that help to determine what is normal for them. Extremes usually indicate a lack of inner balance. Observe it for a time. It may only be temporary and may right itself. If it doesn't, that is the time to evaluate the situation to see if special help may be indicated.

ALL FUNERAL PROFESSIONALS NEED TO BE CAREFUL WITH REFERRALS FOR IT WOULD BE EASY FOR A PERSON TO BE OFFENDED IF IT IS NOT DONE WISELY.

It would never be proper in a funeral home to walk up to a person and say, "I think you need a psychiatrist." Things have to be done much more delicately.

If a person seems to be excessively disturbed and you observe it, and others do not seem to notice it, it might be wise to speak to a member of the family or the pastor. You might say something like, "John mentioned to me that he felt like giving up on life. Then he said he had an aunt kill herself once. I am concerned about him because he seems to be taking things so hard. It may be his grief expressing itself, but you can never tell. Things like this are too serious to ignore. What do you think would be the wise thing for us to do about it?" This shares the responsibility, alerts others and can lead to protective action.

If it is a lonely person and there seems to be no one with whom you could share responsibility, a more direct approach should be taken. For instance, a deeply disturbed widow might be spoken to in this way, "I sense how deeply you are suffering. Certainly, there must be some way to relieve your suffering and people who can help you. If there is anything I can do, please understand that I can connect you with helpful people. If you want to see someone, I can recommend some great people and I myself would be glad to talk to you – I won't have answers, but I am a good listener. I don't like to see you suffering so much, so if there is anything that I can do to help bring a measure of relief, I'm very willing."

I have used this approach and instead of being offended, the person will usually appreciate your concern and response to your efforts at helpfulness. After this process, it is well to simply wait patiently for a response. Remember: a person's initial response to a referral may well be negative, but in time may well be accepted as a positive.

AFTERCARE PROGRAMS – PRACTICAL THOUGHTS

Within the last several years, numerous funeral homes across the nation have embraced the concept of aftercare, which is always a good thing.

The mission of these programs are admirable, but before entering into an aftercare program all funeral homes should evaluate the program based on three simple criteria:

- Time
- Training
- Expense

These are some legitimate issues which must be considered before starting into any aftercare program.

TIME

Think of this example about time. There are 365 days in a year. If you have a 150-call business, giving two days for each service, you are busy 300 days a year (sometimes night and day). If you add just 50 pre-need conferences to this, plus social, family, and civic responsibilities to your schedule, when will you, the funeral director, have time to make such "post funeral" calls?

If you suffer from burn out, you're of little value to yourself, let alone anyone else.

TRAINING

Words like "therapist," or "therapy" and the like truly connote people who have Ph.D.'s, have completed doctoral programs, or who are graduates of seminaries or law schools.

Due to this reality, funeral professionals who use terms like "therapist" or "therapy" are at risk for future litigation.

Attorney colleagues of mine in funeral service admonish the funeral professional to be careful in the area of aftercare and stay away from risky titles and labels.

EXPENSE

Aftercare programs can be expensive, but they need not be. If a funeral home hires a full-time counselor, the expenses need not to be enumerated here. Everyone in management knows how expensive payroll and employee benefit programs are. Even part-time counselors are an expense and often, they are not very reliable or permanent.

Aftercare programs in the funeral home environment should at minimum be a program which will do the following:

- Respect the funeral director's busy schedule.
- Be economic.
- Be effective.
- Have low liability risks.
- Be reasonable in expectations and outcomes.

UNIQUE SITUATIONS IN FUNERAL COUNSELING

In my experience in funeral counseling, three specific situations seem to arise with such a regular consistency that each one needs to be addressed specifically. They are:

I. Professionals who are opposed to funerals.
II. Bringing children to funerals.
III. Split and fractured family units.

I. PROFESSIONALS WHO ARE OPPOSED TO FUNERALS

It probably amazes every funeral professional in the world that certain other professional people, (some clergy, some teachers, most media people, etc.) are opposed to funerals.

Most funeral professionals have stood in amazement when a clergy for instance will endorse, encourage, and engage flowers at a wedding as being a good idea, but when it comes to funeral flowers – they declare it is such a waste; even though the flowers at both weddings and funerals all end up dead.

I well remember when a young person killed himself with a drug overdose and in an attempt at crisis intervention, the school asked me to address the students. When I arrived at the school, the principal, a professional educator, warned me, "Don't talk about death and morbid stuff too much."

Funeral counseling can and does come to a stop when the purity of the funeral experience is challenged by these kinds of situations and reactions. And as blatantly contradictory as endorsing wedding rituals and scorning funeral rituals is, it happens all the time.

Is there anything that we can do to help other professional people who are opposed to funerals, but who are consistently in a position to be confronted with funerals? I think there is.

It is very important in the beginning to try to understand the roots of the opposition. Usually when a person exhibits trouble with funerals it is because he or she has a lot of death anxiety. Just as funeral directors have had bad experiences with other professional people, sometimes the root of the problem is that the professional people have had bad experiences with funeral directors.

In either instance, some things that are constructive can be done. Many people have had their minds changed by getting the facts in a wider perspective. All funeral professionals can try by their own behavior and attitude to make up for the bad experiences of the past and to make sure that as far as they are concerned, that will never happen again.

When death anxiety exists, people need help to resolve it. Usually this anxiety is caused by a diffused fear that is not easily brought into focus. Often just talking about things can help to bring the fears into the open and help to resolve them. At other times, accurate information can take the place of misinformation and a new point-of-view can help to see things differently.

During the last three decades or so, I have given seminars to more than 20,000 clergy of all faiths and have found them to be reasonable, concerned, and actively seeking the truth about funerals when it was made available. There is a tremendous amount of good and honest information available - all that needs to happen is for us to get about the task of getting this information out before these good people are confronted with a death situation both literally and professionally. It is critically important that funeral professionals tell their story.

CASE STUDY: "TELL YOUR STORY"

I was giving a clergy seminar to a group of about 80 clergy in a middle-size town in a southern state.

The seminar was a long one. It went from 9:00 a.m. to 4:00 p.m. I felt well prepared and the subject was going to be on the value of rites, rituals and ceremonies at the time of death.

I started out at 9:00 a.m. In the front row there was a clergyman who I could tell was not liking or appreciating me or my message. At 9:10 a.m., he stood up and exclaimed, "Young man you are overstating your case." He continued, "If a person has a great faith then they will handle death all right. They don't need funerals or a funeral director and, in fact, funerals are pagan. Naturally, the undertaker would be in favor of funerals!"

Then he sat down. I was dumbfounded and humiliated. Then I was terrified for I realized I had five hours and fifty minutes to go with this group. I stopped, froze, stumbled, sputtered and almost cried. Then I remembered what a great teacher of mine told me **- TELL YOUR STORY!**

So I gathered my courage and composure and went on. At the break the funeral director who had invited me to speak came over to comfort me. He told me that the minister had been in town a long time, was well liked, and was a very nice and skilled person - just one thing . . . he hated funerals, and thought funeral directors were crooks. He also explained that this minister had made his pre-arrangements at his funeral home and that it was a direct disposal of the body with no services. Nothing.

Surprisingly, the antagonistic minister attended the entire afternoon session. I presented the material the best I could, but all afternoon I was like a raw nerve just waiting for him to jump on me again. The session ended and the minister left without saying a word.

Two weeks later my funeral director friend called me up to relay that this minister had just revised his pre-arrangements, and had added a period of time when his friends could offer their support to his family.

Such is the power of telling the story of the good works of this great profession and at least one of our six logical steps of the funeral was secure.

CHILDREN

After all the thousands of books, tapes, pamphlets, programs, videos and seminars that have been devoted to the subject of children and funerals over the last 30 years, the question still arises -"Should we bring children to the funeral?"

For those who are familiar with the literature on grief and mourning, the answer is a quick "yes."

It is clear, however, from the frequency of the question that even though we have thousands of pieces of information on the subject of children and funerals, most parents have not or have chosen not to read the materials. This state of affairs is understandable given the immature attitude so many people have concerning loss and death.

In any event, from a funeral counseling perspective, if the child would like to participate in a funeral and he or she are old enough to share in such an event it is probably wise to let them attend. If they do not want to come, it is usually a sign that they have already acquired some anxiety about death and this should be worked through carefully. It is never wise to force a child to attend a funeral or wake.

However, on the other hand if they are included in other family activities it would be natural to let them share in the funeral. It can be an important learning experience for them.

Children are responsive to emotional happenings in the family. Their factual knowledge of the world is very limited but their feeling capacity about the world is limitless. They may not understand all that is going on, but they do feel a part of whatever it is.

When there is some kind of ceremony children naturally want to be part of it because they love happenings. They need not be expected to understand it all. For example a little girl can be a flower girl at a wedding without understanding all about adult sex and the responsibilities of marriage.

Likewise a child can attend a funeral without understanding all about loss and death. Yet, if and when they are excluded, children are apt to think something is wrong. Their imaginations go to work which often create a more stressful and exaggerated reality than the death event itself.

They pick up anxiety rather than the healthy attitude that we would like to communicate. Therefore, in most instances it is wise to offer to include children rather than to exclude them. If they are too young to attend the more formal service, it might be possible to go to the funeral home at a time when there is no service. They can see the beautiful flowers, sense the quiet dignity of the setting, see the casket with the deceased prepared for viewing, and have their questions answered in a simple, honest manner. Then rather than being filled with anxiety, they may well gain the idea that death is something that can be wisely managed. They see a role model in mourning practices.

With children, as with adults, it is important to remember that an honest fear of death can help them to protect and preserve life. Having emotional anxiety, however, about death may lead to unwise and life-threatening behavior that is designed to test the boundaries of life and often injure life in the process. It may be that death anxiety planted in early childhood leads to drug use, reckless driving, and death-defying games like "chicken" and "Russian roulette."

CASE STUDY: *In 1975, a very elderly woman died. She was a maiden woman and left only one great nephew as a relative. He lived in the same town with his wife and two daughters, ages four and six.*

The nephew came to the funeral home and made arrangements. His main question was whether or not his two daughters should see their deceased great-great aunt.

I assured him that it would be all right if the girls came to the funeral home and even sighted some literature for him, but he was reserved. Naturally he did not want his two daughters to experience any harm.

We finished all the preparation work and had the deceased great-aunt lying in state in the funeral home chapel. That afternoon, the nephew called up and said that he, and his wife and the girls were going to come over to the funeral home to see the dead body.

I was out in the parking lot when they arrived and as they got out of the car, the mother had a few more questions to ask before they went in to see their aunt.

As we stood there deeply engrossed in adult talking, the two little girls got impatient and asked their mother if they could go walk to the front of the funeral home and wait at the front door. *The mother gave her approval and off the little ones went, while we adults kept on talking and talking and talking.*

Unbeknownst to us was that while we were gabbing about psychology, the two little girls had gone on into the funeral home alone. They walked right into the Chapel, went up to the casket, took a long look at their dead great-great aunt, and returned to the front porch of the funeral home.

As the father, mother and I walked to the front of the building, the two sisters were just sitting on the steps watching the world go by. The mother leaned over to the girls and told them that after a long discussion and for their own well-being the decision had been made to let them go inside and see "Aunt Amanda." The older sister looked up at her mother and said, "Oh, we've already been in there and seen her. Mommy let's go home."
I felt like an idiot.

IT IS ALWAYS WISE TO INCLUDE CHILDREN IN THE LIFE EVENTS OF THE FAMILY STRUCTURE.

FRACTURED FAMILIES

For a half of a century the divorce rate has been hovering at around 50 percent. Thousands of families must wade through the negative phase of adolescence where stress and problems abound. Money problems cause stress, people get disillusioned, and children rarely have a parent at home after school. As attractive as the ideal is of the family structure seen on television with "The Walton's" and "7th Heaven," the reality of family life is much different.

Since the funeral ritual reflects everything about human life, both good and bad, no one should be surprised that dysfunctional families cause tension and difficulties in both arranging and executing funerals.

Most human situations inevitably involve conflicts. Sometimes it is divorce, separation, cheating, drug use or alcoholism. Sometimes it is a family squabble that has kept people apart. When death comes, their feelings are bound to be projected into the funeral process.

What can be done? Sometimes the funeral process can restore communication that can lead to a healing of wounds, this is an ideal. Sometimes the compassion of the moment brings people together in such a way that old enmities are put aside out of respect for the mutual experience of death and grief. There is always a risk – no guarantees.

When it does not seem possible to bring about this form of healing of angry feelings, it is sometimes wise to work out two separate services to be held to meet the needs of the fractured group. This takes some work, but it has been done many times, and successfully!

CASE STUDY: *I received a death call early one morning from a man whose mother had just died. After the initial first call we made an appointment for the next morning. I detected* *nothing unique in my initial contact. When the son and his wife arrived at the funeral home, the situation changed dramatically. The son confided to me that his oldest brother was a criminal on the run and that his crimes had been very serious and that the family was terrified that he would secretly find his way to the funeral and they were very apprehensive as to the consequences.*

After a lengthy discussion, more distressing facts emerged concerning this man's erratic lifestyle. After I gained more information, I myself was uneasy as to the potential happenings over the next four days.

Upon the request of the family, I contacted the County Sheriff who immediately conceded agreement as to the potential danger of the black sheep brother. The Sheriff took the position that the brother was not to be allowed in the county, and because the brother's photo was prominently displayed in the post office lobby the Sheriff notified the Federal Bureau of Investigation.

The calling hours commenced with plain clothed Sheriff Officers throughout the mortuary. Nothing happened. On the day of the funeral, precisely in the middle of the service, the criminal brother marched down the center aisle of the church and sat right by his brother who had made the arrangements.

The entire church was stunned, the minister stopped and within second's law enforcement officers with weapons drawn had surrounded him. The criminal's brother whispered something to his younger brother; they both started crying, embraced each other and the brother gave himself up to the County Sheriff. They put him in handcuffs on the spot. Before they removed him from the sanctuary, they allowed him to lean over and kiss his mother goodbye.

Later, the younger brother told me that his brother had told him that on his mother's grave he would turn himself in and take his due punishment. He said that he could not bear the idea of his mother looking down at him from heaven and see all the terrible things he was doing.

It was a beautiful experience which is an example of how death and funeral ceremonies can transform a person's life.

OF COURSE, NOT ALL FUNERALS WORK OUT SO INSPIRINGLY.

CASE STUDY: *This is a situation that happened in the winter of 1979. I received a death call late one evening notifying me that an elderly man had died at his residence. When we arrived at the house to make the removal, I learned that there were fourteen children surviving, and that a twenty-year-old feud based on divorces, cheating, stealing, alcohol, drugs, lying, and much more was still raging in force. In fact, the sides were drawn seven against seven.*

There were seven pro-father children and seven pro-mother children. The mother had died fifteen years previously in another town.

As I sat down with the seven pro-father children, I was told that under no circumstances did they want to set sight on any of the seven pro-mother children.

After a lengthy conversation, it was determined that we would have staggered hours for each group. For example, from 1-4 p.m. would be calling hours for the pro-mother group, and from 6-9 p.m. would be for the pro-father group. Two separate funeral services would be held. For mother's group the services would be held at 9:00 a.m.; the father's group at 10:30 a.m. There would even be two graveside services. That night it snowed three feet.

The wishes of the family were executed flawlessly, even though the obituary was very long and very complicated. Everything went fine until the trip to the cemetery. The committals were scheduled for the first group at 11:30 a.m., and the second group at noon. As I drove through the gates of the cemetery with the 11:30 a.m. pro-mother group, I saw with great surprise that the noon pro-father group was already standing around the grave. Even the minister I was driving looked fearful. There was no turning back and as I got out of the lead car, I could see several pro-father children hopping through the snow yelling profanities at the pro-mother group.

I tried, in vain, to bring some resemblance of peace to the group as did the minister when all of the sudden out of the blue a snowball was thrown and hit one of the older daughters square in her face. Then the largest snowball fight ensued that I had ever witnessed. The minister and I just sat in the lead car in absolute quiet watching helplessly as this ridiculous site unfolded before our eyes.

Years of repressed and suppressed emotions were being expressed. After about twenty minutes both groups were exhausted and the first group left to wait their turn for the committal. They never made up, the area around the grave looked like a tornado had gone by, and with all this drama finally the original plan was executed.

ASSESSMENT

One of the most fascinating aspects is the uniqueness of each and every interaction. Funeral professionals possess special abilities as organizational specialists and are well versed at bringing order to chaos. Funeral professionals are asked to face up to some of the most unique, special and yes, sometimes distasteful occurrences in a community and they do so with tact, gentleness, dignity and honor.

THE DISTINCTIVE TRAITS OF FUNERAL SERVICE COUNSELING

OUR RESPONSIBILITY

As a member of a caregiving, caretaking and a care-providing profession, funeral directors not only have the right but the obligation to counsel and advice bereaved families. Funeral directors touch the lives of people in their time of greatest need. Our sensitivity to the needs of the bereaved may have a significant bearing on their health and well-being for years to come. The funeral director is a staple in the community; a wise counselor who takes responsibility seriously, is understanding and skilled in human relationships.

In funeral counseling, a knowledge of psychology is extremely important, for counseling is applied psychology. There are two types of psychological knowledge. Usually they complement each other. One is practical knowledge about people and how they function. The other is formal knowledge that is usually learned in the classroom. Both are important for they tend to support each other.

Funeral directors, because of their vast experiences with people in crisis develop a body of information and observations about people that is important - we call this experiential expertise. This learning from experiences has been of great value to those funeral directors who have a warm, responsive nature and who tend to do the right things in a death crisis because of their basic concern for people.

Many compassionate and sensitive funeral directors, and especially younger ones, want to get the benefit of others' experiences because in a time of rapid change they feel they cannot afford the long, slow process of learning by experience. These persons seek to increase their understanding through reading and classroom work which is readily accessible through mortuary colleges, colleges, professional school, workshops, and seminars.

No one in a community has more knowledge and experience in dealing wisely with the death crisis situation than the funeral director. Because of the critical and important nature of the work, communities expect and have a right to expect that in times of crisis they can go to a professionally competent funeral director for counsel and advice.

THE RESPONSIBILITY OF FUNERAL COUNSELING IS OF PARAMOUNT IMPORTANCE.

Here and there the objection is made by funeral directors that they are not counselors, and do not believe in counseling. This may be understandable, but it does not work. Even funeral directors who claim not to counsel, are actually counseling. There really is no choice in the matter. Whenever a funeral director works with people in a time of crisis then they automatically become a counselor. The only choice we have is whether or not we will be a wise and helpful counselor.

To reject the responsibility of counseling is tantamount to saying that there is a part of your role you want to avoid and this is the same thing as saying that you are content to remain an incomplete funeral director. When persons come to us seeking options, suggestions, insights and answers to questions that are important to them and the response is "I simply am here to take your service order and sell you something," that person is missing an important opportunity to serve and the family will rightfully feel awkward and defensive.

Much of funeral counseling is listening. The wise funeral counselor is willing to listen for he or she knows that many people resolve their problems by the very process of putting their thoughts and feelings into words. They gain new perspective by listening to their own ideas as they express them to another and gauge their response. It is also rude not to want to listen to another, especially in time of great need.

As most funeral directors are well aware, time can be a critical issue in funeral counseling. But it is well to remember that not all time is the same. At least emotional time is relative. In times of crises there may be very rapid emotional activity. To be there at this important time is advantageous. The funeral director is with the family during prime time as far as a counseling opportunity is concerned. So, it is not a matter of whether the funeral conference or funeral service lasts a half-hour or five hours, what is important is how well you are prepared to use this prime time to the best advantage of the family served. There are three aspects which needs attention:

First, you need to have a genuine desire to help people and be willing to give the time and effort required to improve your skill.

Second, you need to study. Most colleges have courses in counseling. If you cannot easily access a college, there are courses you can take online courses as well as many useful books in libraries. Also reading a variety of case histories in professional journals is important, for this tells you what people are like and how they react to life crises.

Third, you need to practice. Make as many funeral arrangements as possible. Perhaps there is nothing like actually working with people to make you sensitive to how they respond. Here it is important to go back over your conversations to see where you might also have done things more wisely and sensitively.

One last thought on responsibility: there is a risk in promoting yourself as a grief counselor or grief therapist. In the funeral service profession there exists an unspoken sense of professional humility that usually makes it wise to avoid fancy titles. If a funeral director knows what he or she is doing that is the all-important thing. Often people resist counseling if they know that is what is going on, but welcome it if they feel it is a friendly conversation with a concerned friend. In funeral counseling, the process is the important thing, not the name that is given to it.

The beauty of the funeral is that it does at least four specific things which are available to everyone.

1. **It provides acting out ceremonies that give expression to feelings too deep to be put into words.** The funeral is the most accessible and most adequate resource for this purpose, and the most

economical. The funeral has the great advantage of being generally understood, and of possessing within its process, the resources for meeting the varied social, emotional, and spiritual needs of the bereaved. Each step of the way has its own built-in wisdom to assist people in making thoughtful decisions during the crisis of death.

2. **It provides the framework for group support. It makes it possible for people to get together, to visit, to communicate and to relate to each other.** It provides many ways by which people can express love and concern and makes people feel comfortable in doing what would otherwise be more distressing. There is a risk in judging whom and who will not be affected by a death; too old, no friends, too young, no friends is a fragile position in which to make once in a lifetime decisions.

3. **It encourages the expression of feelings.** The whole funeral process is a feeling oriented activity. Feelings are so important that they need to be recognized and expressed.

4. **The funeral provides values to live by.** It confirms the value of life in the presence of death. It not only shows respect for the dead, but also for the living. Each funeral carries with it a challenge to a new and better life.

These four points then challenge the idea that the customer is always right concerning the funeral. Knowledge of the death crisis is necessary for healthy bereavement. The conviction of belief in the benefits of the funeral communicated to everyone by the funeral director can and does help direct poorly thought ideas and decisions into healthier and more meaningful channels.

Hinging on the future of the funeral is the funeral director's own belief in what he or she does, and an adherence to the issue of confirming the reality of death in the minds of the bereaved.

Viewing dead people has somewhat fallen out of the vogue over the last few years. This is not only unfortunate but can be tragic as well. Much of the future of funeral service counseling pivots on re-embracing this vital form of psychological knowledge.

So why all the fuss about facing reality when many claim they know it already? It is important here to realize that knowing has many levels. If the state police call and ask your daughter's name, make of car and registration number, and then tells you that she has been killed in a highway accident, you know the fact. That is, you understand the words that were spoken to you. You know how to put them together in a sentence and understand what the sentence meant. But the kind of knowing that is involved in funeral counseling is much deeper. It is so deep that other parts of your being may instantly be stimulated to say, "It can't be so." There is a great difference between verbal meaning and emotional meaning. The system needs a variety of events to confirm the verbal reality beyond all emotional denial. The funeral provides that variety of acting out procedures that speak to the total being, mind, reason, feelings, and spirit. It is this larger form of knowing that the funeral is all about.

Much of the future of this great profession is dependent upon the willingness of funeral directors to consistently expand their counseling skills and the helping network of the funeral home. This seems to be a most admirable and attainable professional goal.

CASE STUDY:

I received a call in 1981 to care for a young mother who had experienced a neonatal death. When I arrived at the hospital, the mother was still unable to be seen and so I spoke with her husband.

This young man was trying his best to be "in control." He announced that since no one knew the baby, and since the baby was not even a live birth, he felt strongly that the body should be disposed of as quickly as possible. Then he looked straight at me and announced that he did not want his wife involved with anything. She was to know as little as possible about what happened.

I listened to him until he was completely exhausted and then began to ask him some questions. "What was the last funeral you attended?" "What did you find helpful about that experience?" He responded that it was helpful to see his family and friends. Then, I asked about his parents and his wife's parents. After a time, I shared some information about things that might be important to his wife. I think we spoke to each other for about five hours and throughout this process, he experienced a change in attitude.

Ten days later, after his wife was able to leave the hospital and felt physically better, we had a funeral in a church, with flowers and lots of people. In fact, it proved to be one of the largest funerals I ever conducted.

Even from the least of these, the long arm effect of grief expressed itself. The parents had legions of friends as did the grandparents. Everyone really wanted to say goodbye and through the wise and careful management of the funeral this was accomplished.

It was my responsibility as a funeral professional to do so.

ASSESSMENT

Funeral directors take their responsibility to care for the dead and the living very seriously; few vocations carry such a heavy burden. Responsibility in funeral service can easily be witnessed by the numbers of years the average funeral home has been servicing their communities. Funeral firms with service heritages of 50, 75, 100 or even 150 years are not uncommon. Such numbers imply that a responsible funeral professional was and is at work.

THE FUTURE

Much of the future of funeral counseling will depend on the funeral director's ability to adapt and initiate new types of services which fill the needs of new types of people's expectations.

We live in a time of rapid change and this trend shows no signs of abating. People move about the country and learn to do things differently. Hence, it is critical to make possible the types of services that have meaning and value to the various types of people who are involved. The Roman Catholic Church has a new funeral ritual, new types of national and ethnic communities are scattered throughout North America, people have embraced cremation as a conviction, more and more people are unchurched and the list of changes concerning funeral service goes on and on.

The important thing is to have valid services that can and do serve psychological needs. Just because a person is young or old, a believer or a nonbeliever, wants cremation over burial, should not determine whether or not they should be denied the benefits of the funeral process. Rather, some form of meaningful service should be made accessible for everyone. Some of the new types of services do this very well. Be creative for this is where new ideas emerge.

A word of caution: some types of service innovations may work in the opposite direction. Some services recommended by some agencies and thinkers tend to reduce the funeral process and eliminate some of its most significant and therapeutic parts. This can be hazardous for bereaved people and deny them what is needed most in the time of crisis. Such "abridged" funerals reduce the basic benefits of the funeral, taking all that we have learned to be psychologically "unsound," and putting it together in one package. This does not make sense for it leads to the immediate disposal decision.

In funeral counseling, it is important to try to find out what lies behind the request for an immediate disposal of the body without any of the proven psychological benefits of the funeral process. Some people have the mistaken idea that if they have no funeral, or numb themselves with drugs or alcohol, they will avoid any grief. Others have the idea that by quick disposal they will avoid expense. Still others may have done anticipatory grief work over a long period of time and when the person finally dies they feel no need for any of the funeral process. All of these possibilities have limitations.

There exists funeral directors who tell families, when they request immediate disposal, that it is their practice to have a funeral for all bodies entrusted to them. If the family did not want to plan it or participate in it that was up to them, but as a funeral director he explained he could not stay in this type of profession if they did not believe in the funeral. These funeral directors have found that in nearly every case, after a few hours the family would call to inquire about the time of the service and to ask if friends and family could attend. In most cases the people became engaged in the complete funeral process.

Now these funerals consisted simply of this: reciting the name of the deceased, giving his or her birthdate and death date, acknowledging that he or she lived life and a brief conclusion about the fragility and worth of every human life. Then the body was conveyed to the crematory, cemetery or medical school.

No chapel, no flowers, no music, but a funeral none the less. Most of the families wrote this funeral director to thank him for being so considerate and for believing so much in what he did for a living. He was never chastised for his stance, but on the contrary he was recommended as one who really cared about people! This is called professional conviction. What this funeral director did was to make the funeral process available because he believed in it, and then people found themselves wanting to share in it because his belief convinced them of the value of what he did. Any funeral director could employ this conviction of belief in funeral counseling.

CONCLUSION

Ah, the ticking of the clock – tick, tock, tick tock. The hands of time march forward, never backward. Tick, tock, tick tock.

The future comes to each of us with a simple ticking of the clock.

Inscribed on a sundial at Oxford University are the Latin words "Periunt et Impurtanture," meaning "the hours perish and are laid to your charge."

Learning funeral counseling takes time, actual funeral counseling takes time, and the rituals of death take time – time then is an essential ingredient in our beloved profession.

For your families' benefit and your own professional growth, devote all the time you can afford to our professions noble mission which is to minister and assist in alleviating some of the pain from grief that our families, friends and neighbors confront and experience as they "walk through the valley of the shadow of death."

Our profession's ancient call us to assist the bereaved in a counseling relationship is truly a most admirable and worthy thing to do.

ABOUT THE AUTHOR

Todd W. Van Beck has been serving the funeral profession for fifty years. He started his career at the Heafey & Heafey Mortuary in Omaha, Nebraska and throughout his career has been involved with every aspect of the purpose, meaning and benefit of funeral rituals and ceremonies, as well as the subjects of death, grief, bereavement care, funeral service history, as well as management issues in funeral service. Mr. Van Beck is an author, teacher, lecturer on an international basis. He has published over 600 professional articles as well as having written over 60 training programs. His book "Winning Ways" was published in 1998, and most recently he has published two new books, "Reverence for the Dead" and "The Story of Cremation." He was honored by the ICCFA Educational Foundation with their first "Landmark Career" award in 2014. Mr. Van Beck also holds an honorary doctorate degree from the Commonwealth Institute of Funeral Service. He is currently on the staff of the John A. Gupton College, in Nashville, Tennessee. He is married to Georgia who is a Clinical Supervisor with Hospice.

Made in the USA
Monee, IL
05 January 2021